At Issue

| The Right to a Living Wage

Other Books in the At Issue Series

At Issue

The Right to a Living Wage

Matt Uhler, Book Editor

WITHDRAWN

Published in 2018 by Greenhaven Publishing, LLC
353 3rd Avenue, Suite 255, New York, NY 10010

Copyright © 2018 by Greenhaven Publishing, LLC

First Edition

Articles in Greenhaven Publishing anthologies are often edited for length to meet page
requirements. In addition, original titles of these works are changed to clearly present
the main thesis and to explicitly indicate the author's opinion. Every effort is made to
ensure that Greenhaven Publishing accurately reflects the original intent of the authors.
Every effort has been made to trace the owners of the copyrighted material.

Cover image: Lightspring/Shutterstock.com

Library of Congress Cataloging-in-Publication Data
Names: Uhler, Matt, editor.
Title: The right to a living wage / Matt Uhler, book editor.
Description: First edition. | New York : Greenhaven Publishing, 2018. |
  Series: At issue | Includes bibliographical references and index. | Audience: Grades
  7-12.
Identifiers: LCCN 2017009713| ISBN 9781534500822 (library bound) | ISBN
9781534500808 (pbk.)
Subjects: LCSH: Minimum wage--United states--Juvenile literature. | Living
  wage movement--United States--Juvenile literature.
Classification: LCC HD4918 .R54 2018 | DDC 331.2/3--dc23
LC record available at https://lccn.loc.gov/2017009713

Manufactured in the United States of America

Website: http://greenhavenpublishing.com

Contents

Introduction

Congress established the minimum wage in 1938 with the passage of the Fair Labor Standards Act. The first minimum wage was 25 cents an hour, and the current minimum wage is $7.25 an hour. The first minimum wage was limited to select industries and gradually expanded to the nearly universal coverage that it sees today.

The first living wage ordinances came into being in the United States in Baltimore in 1994. By comparison, living wage ordinances tend to be restricted to companies under contract with a local government, higher than the national minimum wage, and set at levels to guarantee that a family reaches or exceeds the poverty level. The right to a living wage has been debated for decades—with much of that debate centered on the economic impact of the minimum wage and the costs associated with raising that standard. The goal of both minimum wage legislation and living wage ordinances is to raise the wages of low-income workers as a means of alleviating poverty.

In 2014, the U.S. Senate debated the Minimum Wage Fairness Act, which proposed to increase the minimum wage to $10.10 an hour in three incremental steps over the course of two years. President Barack Obama strongly supported increasing the federal minimum wage, and numerous public polls show wide support among citizens for an increase to the minimum wage. In opposition to increasing wages is the argument that prices will increase and jobs will be lost. The Congressional Budget Office (CBO) estimated that approximately 500,000 jobs would be lost if the minimum wage were to be increased to $10.10. The CBO also estimated that increasing the minimum wage to $10.10 and tying it to inflation would increase the wages of 16.5 million workers in 2016. Currently, there are 29 states that have minimum wages set higher than the federal minimum. Additionally, several cities have ordinances that exceed the federal minimum, most notably San Francisco, Seattle, Washington, DC, Los Angeles, and New York.

Adjusted for inflation, the minimum wage peaked in terms of buying power in 1968. According to the Pew Research Center, the federal minimum wage has lost about 9.6% of its purchasing power since it was last increased in 2009. What ties the living wage movement to the minimum wage movement is the notion that working families and individuals should be able to cover the cost of their most basic needs. It is argued that when the buying power of the minimum wage declines, families struggle to meet those needs. Critics of wage floors argue that minimum wages primarily effect teens and would have little benefit to working families.

Over the course of recent U.S. election cycles, there has been a increased effort to push minimum wages to the $15-an-hour mark. Critics argue that such a significant increase will not only cost jobs, but will cause economic stagnation at a time when greater economic stimulus is needed. Proponents of higher wages argue that, by putting money in the hands of low-wage earners, consumer spending will rise, which in turn will boost the overall economy and create jobs. Many of the viewpoints in *At Issue: The Right to a Living Wage* examine this compelling and crucial economic debate.

1

Increasing Pay Has Its Ups and Downs

John Wihbey

John Wihbey is assistant director for Journalist's Resource at the Harvard Kennedy School's Shorenstein Center on Media, Politics, and Public Policy.

The long-standing debate over minimum wage legislation involves economic modeling at the national and local levels, both of which can have broad effects on inflation, the job market, and the American workplace. Numerous studies have been launched by economists and scientists alike, researching the impact of raising minimum wage on rising costs and job growth—with the consensus being that there are trade-offs between higher wages and job losses but not necessarily any evidence of correlation.

In 2016, California became the first state to adopt legislation that will gradually raise the minimum wage to $15 per hour. New York City, Seattle, and Washington D.C. also have plans to phase in a $15-per-hour wage floor. Others are raising wages above the federally mandated rate, according to the National Conference of State Legislators. On August 1, 2016, for example, Minnesota's minimum wage rose to $9.50 per hour at the state's largest companies.

The changes come after years of national debate about the need to raise pay so families can earn a living wage. The U.S.

"Minimum wage: Updated research roundup on the effects of increasing pay", by John Wihbey, July, 27, 2016. http://journalistsresource.org/studies/economics/inequality/the-effects-of-raising-the-minimum-wage. Licensed under CC BY 3.0.

federal minimum wage was first established during the Depression, and it has risen from 25 cents to $7.25 per hour since it was first instituted in 1938 as part of the Fair Labor Standards Act. Despite the increases, inflation has eroded its value; returning it to the value it held in 1968 would require an increase to nearly $10 per hour. In his 2013 State of the Union address, President Obama called for raising the minimum wage to $9 per hour, which in adjusted terms would put it back at its early 1980s level. According to administration estimates, this would boost the wages of some 15 million people. Supporters of these efforts note that women in particular are likely to benefit significantly.

But increasing the minimum wage may have impacts beyond adding more money to employees' pockets. A Purdue University study released in July 2015 suggests that paying fast-food restaurant employees $15 an hour could lead to higher prices. Prices at those businesses could increase by an estimated 4.3 percent, according to the report.

Earlier studies have indicated that some businesses will cut jobs to pay employees more. In February 2014, the nonpartisan Congressional Budget Office issued a report, "The Effects of a Minimum-Wage Increase on Employment and Family Income," that explores two scenarios: Raising the minimum wage to $10.10 or to $9.00. The report concludes that there are distinct trade-offs. Under the $10.10 scenario, there would likely be a reduction of about 500,000 workers across the labor market, as businesses shed jobs, but about 16.5 million low-wage workers would see substantial gains in their earnings in an average week. Under the $9.00 scenario, the labor force would see a reduction of 100,000 jobs, but an estimated 7.6 million low-wage workers would see a boost in their weekly earnings.

Critics assert that the real effects of minimum-wage increases are negative: they hurt businesses, raise prices and ultimately are counterproductive for the working poor, as they can lead to unemployment. For a good sense of the partisan argument—and the statistics and studies that are often cited—see these position pieces from the right-leaning American Enterprise Institute and the left-leaning Center for American Progress.

At the macro level, a substantial increase in the federal minimum wage is likely to have broad effects, with some studies predicting that it could "ripple" across the economy, boosting the wages of nearly 30 percent of the American workforce.

The best starting point for understanding the debate may be a factual picture of minimum-wage earners, as there are many myths. The U.S. Bureau of Labor Statistics (BLS) illustrates this as follows:

The BLS further notes that in 2015: "Minimum wage workers tend to be young. Although workers under age 25 represented only about one-fifth of hourly paid workers, they made up about half of those paid the federal minimum wage or less. Among employed teenagers (ages 16 to 19) paid by the hour, about 11 percent earned the minimum wage or less, compared with about 2 percent of workers age 25 and older."

There is a huge research literature associated with this issue, as detailed below. Among the extended primers worth considering is the 2014 book *What Does the Minimum Wage Do?* by Dale Belman of Michigan State University and Paul Wolfson of the Tuck School of Business at Dartmouth. That work synthesizes some 200 papers. In their conclusion, they write:

Evidence leads us to conclude that moderate increases in the minimum wage are a useful means of raising wages in the lower part of the wage distribution that has little or no effect on employment and hours. This is what one seeks in a policy tool, solid benefits with small costs. That said, current research does not speak to whether the same results would hold for large increases in the minimum wage.

Fundamentals and Framings

Beneath the political claims and efforts on both sides is a profound philosophical debate between neoclassical economics—with its emphasis on aggregate growth and what is best for the market as a whole—and progressive economics, beginning with John Maynard

Percentage of hourly workers with pay rates at or below federal minimum wage, by characteristic, in 2011

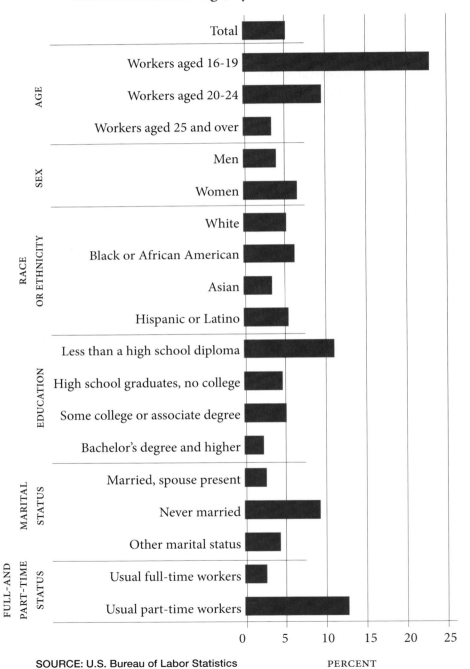

SOURCE: U.S. Bureau of Labor Statistics

PERCENT

Keynes and the New Deal, with an emphasis on shared prosperity and fairness. In the minimum-wage debate, much depends on framing and assumptions, as well as one's interpretation of the larger patterns of increasing wage inequality in the United States. Although there is no doubt that inequality has risen significantly over the past few decades, studies can be found to support positions on both sides of the minimum-wage issue, and questions remain about the precise relationship with inequality dynamics.

Scholarly debates over the minimum wage have taken a distinct shape over the past two decades. In the 1990s, Princeton's Alan Krueger—now Chairman of the White House Council of Economic Advisers—and his colleague David Card produced a seminal paper that has framed much of the subsequent debate. Those scholars examined the results of a New Jersey law raising the minimum wage, comparing the outcomes in the fast food industry to those in the bordering state of Pennsylvania, where wage laws remained the same. Their study called into question textbook assumptions about how labor markets might work. The findings included:

- The data indicated "no evidence that the rise in New Jersey's minimum wage reduced employment at fast-food restaurants in the state."
- Further, "prices of fast-food meals increased in New Jersey relative to Pennsylvania, suggesting that much of the burden of the minimum-wage rise was passed on to consumers."

That paper's implication was that the neoclassical models, which suggested the opposite would happen, didn't comport with reality—data triumphed over theory. For the next decade, the economics profession saw an extended debate about whether that paper's fundamental insights were right and could be extended to support policy. Krueger and Card had to defend their findings in a follow-up to the original paper. In 2000, dozens of pages of an issue of the *American Economic Review* were dedicated to this fight, as Timothy Taylor notes at his "Conversable Economist" blog.

Subsequent Studies

Some subsequent studies have generally supported aspects of Krueger/Card. A 2004 study of available literature, "The Effect of Minimum Wage on Prices," analyzed a wide variety of research on the impact of changes in the minimum wage. The paper, from the University of Leicester, found that firms tend to respond to minimum wage increases not by reducing production or employment, but by raising prices. Overall, price increases are modest: For example, a 10 percent increase in the minimum wage would increase food prices by no more than 4 percent and overall prices by no more than 0.4 percent, significantly less than the minimum-wage increase.

In a 2010 study published in *Review of Economics and Statistics*, scholars Arindrajit Dube, T. William Lester and Michael Reich also looked at low-wage sectors in states that raised the minimum wage and compared them with those in bordering areas where there were no mandated wage changes. They found "strong earnings effects and no employment effects of minimum-wage increases."

A 2012 paper published in the *Journal of Public Economics*, "Optimal Minimum Wage Policy in Competitive Labor Markets," furnishes a theoretical model that lends some support to the empirical insights of Krueger/Card. The paper, from David Lee at Princeton and Emmanuel Saez at UC-Berkeley, concludes: "The minimum wage is a useful tool if the government values redistribution toward low wage workers, and this remains true in the presence of optimal nonlinear taxes/transfers." However, under certain labor market conditions, it may be better for the government to subsidize low-wage workers and keep the minimum wage relatively low.

Diverse Outcomes

The research generally supports the idea that raising the minimum wage would have varying effects across U.S. regions and industries, even if on the whole it doesn't produce massive negative effects.

A 2013 paper for the National Bureau of Economic Research, "Revisiting the Minimum Wage-Employment Debate: Throwing the Baby Out with the Bathwater?" casts doubt on some of the existing research methods and data modeling that economists have used. The paper's authors, which include longtime subject experts David Neumark of the University of California at Irvine and William Wascher of the Federal Reserve Board, find that the overall evidence "still shows that minimum wages pose a tradeoff of higher wages for some against job losses for others, and that policymakers need to bear this tradeoff in mind when making decisions about increasing the minimum wage." These scholars have written previously that, in the short run, minimum wage increases both help some families get out of poverty and make it more likely that previously non-poor families may fall into poverty.

At the ground level, this all suggests that a small firm in a low-wage region might, for example, respond to an increase in the minimum wage by having the owner pick up more hours herself and cut back on an employee's overtime hours. A large firm might likewise try to squeeze more work out of its salaried managers and hire more part-time workers, to avoid benefits obligations. At the same time, because work has a social dimension—and is not purely an economic endeavor—many employees might keep their jobs at the higher mandated wages because of employer loyalty or trust, or the simple desire to avoid the complications of restructuring business operations to account for fewer workers. The lesson here is to distrust sweeping generalizations about what might result from a minimum-wage increase within the national labor market as a whole.

Related Subsidies

It's worth keeping in mind that low wages impact more than just workers. The Earned Income Tax Credit (EITC) is, in effect, a wage subsidy, and consequently paid for by taxpayers, not private firms. A 2013 study from U.C. Berkeley and the University of Illinois at Urbana-Champaign, "Fast Food, Poverty Wages: The Public Cost of Low-wage Jobs in the Fast-Food Industry," found that workers at McDonalds and other major restaurant chains use federal and state programs at far higher rates than other workers—costs that are again picked up by society. A raise in the minimum wage might, in theory, shift some of the burden back to private companies, something that some labor economists see as being only fair.

A 2004 briefing paper from the U.C. Berkeley Labor Center, "Hidden Cost of Wal-Mart Jobs," analyzes this issue through a study of the nation's largest retail employer. As *Washington Post* columnist Ezra Klein has suggested, however, the overall cost-benefit analysis for such retailers must account for more than just wages.

A Helpful Resource

MIT's Living Wage Calculator explains the amount an individual must earn to support oneself and a family across all American states and counties, along with data on expenses, typical annual salaries and local minimum wages. In Manhattan, for example, the living wage for an adult with one child is over $28.24 per hour; it is over $14.52 for a single adult. The local minimum wage is currently $8.75. In Grand Island, Nebraska, the living wage for a single adult is $9.36; with one child $20.81; the minimum wage is $8.

2

Mandating Higher Wages Will Raise Incomes

David Neumark

David Neumark is professor of economics and director of the Center for Economics and Public Policy at the University of California, Irvine.

According to several experts, the goal of wage floors (for both minimum wages and living wages) is to reduce the effects of poverty through gainful and fiscally rewarding employment. This viewpoint provides a brief examination of the effects of minimum wage laws and living wage laws on reducing poverty, making the bold claim that higher wages can ultimately raise incomes across the board but may also prevent companies from hiring low-skill workers—thus negating the good intentions of a better living wage.

A number of policy proposals and initiatives have been used in the United States in an attempt to reduce poverty, or more generally to assist low-income families, by increasing the incomes of families at the bottom end of the income distribution. My research over the recent past has focused on studying the effectiveness of two such policies that mandate higher wages for low-wage workers: minimum wages and living wages. (2)

Minimum wages first were established on a national level with the Fair Labor Standards Act of 1938. While initial coverage was originally quite restrictive, coverage is now nearly universal. The

"Raising Incomes by Mandating Higher Wages", by David Neumark, National Bureau Of Economic Research, Thursday, October 20, 2002. Reprinted by Permission.

federal minimum currently stands at $5.15. Numerous states have at times imposed higher minimum wages, typically for the same workers covered by the federal minimum, but with some exceptions. The highest state minimum wages currently are in California and Massachusetts ($6.75) and Washington ($6.90).

Living wage ordinances are a much more recent innovation. Baltimore was the first city to pass such legislation, in 1994, and approximately 50 cities and a number of other jurisdictions have followed suit. Living wage laws have three central features. First, they impose a wage floor that is higher—and often much higher— than traditional federal and state minimum wages. Second, living wage levels are often explicitly pegged to the wage level needed for a family to reach the federal poverty line. Third, coverage by living wage ordinances is highly restricted. Frequently, cities impose wage floors only on companies under contract (generally including non-profits) with the city. Other cities also impose the wage floor on companies receiving business assistance from the city, in almost every case in addition to coverage of city contractors. Finally, a still smaller number of cities also impose the requirement on themselves and pay city employees a legislated living wage.

It is fair to say that the goal of both minimum wages and living wages is to raise incomes of low-wage workers so as to reduce poverty. Senator Edward Kennedy, a perennial sponsor of legislation to increase the minimum wage, has been quoted as saying "The minimum wage was one of the first-and is still one of the best-anti-poverty programs we have." (3) Similarly, the Economic Policy Institute, while noting that other anti-poverty tools are needed, argues that "the living wage is a crucial tool in the effort to end poverty." (4) Thus, while there is generally no single measure with which the distributional effects of a policy can be assessed unambiguously, and while overall welfare effects are much more complicated, evaluating the impact of mandated wage floors on poverty is quite relevant to the policy debate.

While mandating higher wages for low-wage workers would appear to a non-economist as a natural way to fight poverty, there are two reasons why it may not help to achieve this goal. First, standard economic theory predicts that a mandated wage floor will discourage the use of low-skilled labor, essentially operating as a tax on the use of such labor. Thus, whatever wage gains accrue to workers whose employment is not affected must be offset by the potential earnings losses for some other workers. Second, mandated wage floors may target low-income families ineffectively. Broadly speaking, low-wage workers in the United States belong to two groups. The first is very young workers who have not yet acquired labor market skills, but who are likely to escape low-wage work as skills are acquired. The second is low-skilled adults who are likely to remain mired in low-wage work, (5) and who— as adults—are much more likely to be in poor families. To the extent that the gains from mandated wage floors accrue to low-wage adults and the losses fall on low-wage, non-poor teenagers, mandated wage floors may well reduce poverty. But there is no theoretical reason to believe that this outcome is more likely than the reverse, with concomitant adverse outcomes for low-income families. The distributional effect of mandated wage floors is a purely empirical question.

Minimum Wages

Labor economists have written innumerable papers testing the prediction that minimum wages reduce employment. Earlier studies used aggregate time-series data for the United States to estimate the effects of changes in the national minimum wage. The consensus view from these "first generation" studies was that the elasticity of employment of low-skilled (young) workers with respect to minimum wages was most likely between 0.1 and 0.2; that is, for every ten-percent increase in the minimum wage, employment of low-skilled individuals falls by one to two percent. (6)

More recent studies have used panel data covering multiple states over time, exploiting differences across states in minimum wages. This approach permits researchers to abstract from aggregate economic changes that may coincide with changes in the national minimum wage and hence make difficult untangling the effects of minimum wages in aggregate time-series data. (7) Evidence from these "second generation" studies has spurred considerable controversy regarding whether or not minimum wages reduce employment of low-skilled workers, with some researchers arguing that the predictions of the standard model are wrong, and that minimum wages do not reduce and may even increase employment. The most prominent and often-cited such study uses data collected from a telephone survey of managers or assistant managers in fast-food restaurants in New Jersey and Pennsylvania before and after a minimum wage increase in New Jersey. (8) Not only do these data fail to indicate a relative employment decline in New Jersey, but rather they show that employment rose sharply there (with positive employment elasticities in the range of 0.7).

On the other hand, much recent evidence using similar sorts of data tends to confirm the prediction that minimum wages reduce employment of low-skilled workers; (9) so does earlier work with a much longer panel of states. (10) Moreover, an approach to estimating the employment effects of minimum wages that focuses more explicitly on whether minimum wages are high relative to an equilibrium wage for affected workers reveals two things: first, disemployment effects appear when minimum wages are more likely to be binding (because the equilibrium wage absent the minimum is low); second, some of the small or zero estimated disemployment effects in other studies appear to be from regions or periods in which minimum wages were much less likely to have been binding. (11) Finally, a re-examination of the New Jersey-Pennsylvania study that I conducted, based on payroll records collected from fast-food establishments, finds that the original telephone survey data were plagued by severe measurement error, and that the payroll data generally point to negative employment elasticities. (12)

Across this array of more recent evidence, the estimated effects often parallel the earlier time-series research indicating that the elasticity of employment of low-skilled workers with respect to the minimum wage is in the 0.1 to 0.2 range, with estimates for teenagers (who have often been the focus of minimum wage research) closer to 0.1. As further evidence, a leading economics journal recently published a survey including economists' views of the best estimates of minimum wage effects. Results of this survey, which was conducted in 1996—after most of the recent research on minimum wages was well-known to economists—indicated that the median "best estimate" of the minimum wage elasticity for teenagers was 0.1, while the mean estimate was 0.21. (13) Thus, although there may be some outlying perspectives, economists' views of the effects of the minimum wage are centered in the range of the earlier estimates, and many of the more-recent estimates, of the disemployment effects of minimum wages.

While the research on disemployment effects appears to settle (for many, at least) a question regarding the labor demand effects of mandated wage floors, it does not answer the question of whether minimum wages raise incomes of low-wage workers, or more importantly of poor or low-income families. (14) Turning first to low-wage workers, I recently examined the effects of minimum wages on employment, hours, wages, and ultimately labor income of workers at different points in the wage distribution. (15) This research indicates that workers initially earning near the minimum wage are on net adversely affected by minimum wage increases while, not surprisingly, higher-wage workers are little affected. While wages of low-wage workers increase (although by considerably less than pure contemporaneous effects indicate), their hours and employment decline, and the combined effect of these changes is a decline in earned income. (16)

Finally, while there are few poor or low-income families with high-wage workers, there are many high-income families with low-wage workers. (17) Thus, knowing the effects of minimum wages on low-wage workers does not lead to any firm prediction regarding the effects of minimum wages on poor or low-income families. However, evidence from my recent research utilizing a non-parametric approach to estimating the impact of the minimum wage on the distribution of family income indicates that raising the minimum wage does not reduce the proportion of families living in poverty and, if anything, instead increases it, thus raising the poverty rate. (18) Thus, the combined evidence indicates that minimum wages do not appear to accomplish their principal policy goal of raising incomes of low-wage workers or of poor or low-income families.

One qualification to keep in mind is that this research tends to focus on the short-run effects of minimum wages, typically looking at effects at most a year after minimum wage increases. I am presently working on estimating the longer-run distributional effects of minimum wages. But two sets of existing findings point to some potentially longer-lasting adverse effects of minimum wages—effects that extend beyond disemployment effects, to those who work. First, minimum wages tend to reduce school enrollments of teenagers, at least where these enrollments are not constrained by compulsory schooling laws. (19) Second, extending earlier research on the relationship between minimum wages and on-the-job training, I find in a recent study that minimum wages reduce training that is intended to improve skills on the current job. (20) Thus, minimum wages may reduce the human capital accumulation that leads to higher wages and incomes.

Living Wages

I have recently completed a monograph and a set of papers that analyze many of these same questions with regard to living wage laws. (21) In these papers, paralleling the strategy used in much of the new research on minimum wages, I identify the effects of living wages by comparing changes in labor market outcomes in cities that pass living wages with changes in cities that do not pass such laws.

I begin by asking whether living wage laws may lead to detectable increases in wages at the lower end of the wage or skill distribution. While such effects are readily detectable with respect to minimum wages, the question arises with respect to living wages because of the low fraction of workers covered, and because of questions about enforcement. (22) The evidence points to sizable effects of living wage ordinances on the wages of low-wage workers in the cities in which these ordinances are enacted. In fact, the magnitudes of the estimated wage effects (elasticities of approximately 0.07 for workers in the bottom tenth of the wage distribution) are much larger than would be expected based on the apparently limited coverage of city contractors by most living wage laws. Additional analyses that help reconcile these large effects indicate that the effects are driven by cities in which the coverage of living wage laws is more broad, that is, cities that impose living wages on employers receiving business assistance from the city. (23)

As with minimum wages, the potential gains from higher wages may be offset by reduced employment opportunities. Overall, evidence of disemployment effects is weaker than the evidence of positive wage effects. Nonetheless, disemployment effects tend to appear precisely for the type of living wage laws that generate positive wage effects, in particular, for low-skill workers covered by the broader laws that apply to employers receiving business assistance. Thus, as economic theory would lead us to expect, living wage laws present a trade-off between wages and employment.

This sets the stage for weighing these competing effects, in particular examining the effect of living wage laws on poverty in the urban areas in which they are implemented. Overall, the evidence suggests that living wages may be modestly successful at reducing urban poverty in the cities that have adopted such legislation. In particular, the probability that families have incomes below the poverty line falls in relative terms in cities that pass living wage laws. (24) Paralleling the findings for wage and employment effects, the impact on poverty arises only for the broader living wage laws that cover employers receiving business assistance from cities.

In interpreting this evidence, it is important to keep two things in mind. First, while economic theory predicts that raising mandated wage floors will lead to some employment reductions, it makes no predictions whatsoever regarding the effects of living wages on the distribution of family incomes, or on poverty specifically. The distributional effects depend on both the magnitudes of the wage and employment effects, and on their incidence throughout the family income distribution. Second, and following from this same point, there is no contradiction between the evidence that living wages reduce poverty and that minimum wages increase poverty. The gains and losses from living wages may be of quite different magnitudes, and fall at different points in the distribution of family income than do the gains and losses from minimum wages; this depends in part on the types of workers who are affected by these alternative mandated wage floors. Obviously, though, an important area for future research is to parse out the wage and employment effects of minimum wages and living wages at different points in the distribution of family incomes.

Of course a finding that living wage laws reduce poverty does not necessarily imply that these laws increase economic welfare overall (or vice versa). Living wage laws, like all tax and transfer schemes, generally entail some inefficiencies that may reduce welfare relative to the most efficient such scheme. Finally, there is another reason to adopt a cautious view regarding living wages. As already noted, the effects of living wages appear only for broader living wage laws covering employers receiving business or financial assistance. The narrower contractor-only laws have no detectable effects. This raises a puzzle. Why, despite the anti-poverty rhetoric of living wage campaigns, do they often result in passage of narrow contractor-only laws that may cover a very small share of the workforce?

One hypothesis I explore is that municipal unions work to pass living wage laws as a form of rent-seeking. (25) Specifically, by forcing up the wage for contractor labor, living wage laws reduce (or eliminate) the incentive of cities to contract out work done by their members, and in so doing increase the bargaining power and raise the wages of municipal union workers. There is ample indirect evidence consistent with this, as municipal unions are strong supporters of living wage campaigns. As further evidence,

I explored the impact of living wage laws on the wages of lower-wage unionized municipal workers (excluding teachers, police, and firefighters, who do not face competition from contractor labor). The results indicate that these workers' wages are indeed boosted by living wages. In contrast, living wages do not increase the wages other groups of workers whose wages-according to the rent-seeking hypothesis-should not be affected (such as other city workers, or teachers, police, and firefighters). Thus, even if living wage laws have some beneficial effects on the poor, this last evidence suggests that they may well be driven by motivations other than most effectively reducing urban poverty. While this does not imply that living wages cannot be an effective anti-poverty policy, it certainly suggests that they deserve closer scrutiny before strong conclusions are drawn regarding their effectiveness.

Notes

2. Most of my research on minimum wages was done in collaboration with William Wascher, and more recently with Mark Schweitzer as well. Most of my work on living wages was done in collaboration with Scott Adams.
3. A. Clymer, *Edward M. Kennedy: A Biography*, New York: William Morrow & Co, 1999.
4. See www.epinet.org/Issueguides/livingwage/livingwagefaq.html.
5. See W. J. Carrington and B. C. Fallick, "Do Some Workers Have Minimum Wage Careers?" *Monthly Labor Review*, (May 2001) pp. 17-27.
6. For a review of the earlier time-series studies, see C. Brown, C. Gilroy, and A. Kohen "The Effect of the Minimum Wage on Employment and Unemployment," *Journal of Economic Literature*, 20 (2) (June 1982), pp. 487-528. Results extending this research through the mid-1980s and finding more modest effects are reported in A. J. Wellington, "Effects of the Minimum Wage on the Employment Status of Youths: An Update," *Journal of Human Resources*, 26 (1) (Winter 1991), pp. 27-46. A more recent time-series study using data through 1993 and employing more sophisticated tools of time-series analysis finds stronger disemployment effects; see N. Williams and J. A. Mills, "The Minimum Wage and Teenage Employment: Evidence from Time Series," *Applied Economics*, 33 (3) (February 2001), pp. 285-300.
7. See, for example, D. Card, "Using Regional Variation in Wages to Measure the Effects of the Federal Minimum Wage," NBER Working Paper No. 4058, April 1992, and in *Industrial and Labor Relations Review*, 46 (1) (October 1992), pp. 22-37; D.Card, "Do Minimum Wages Reduce Employment? A Case Study of California, 1987-1989," NBER Working Paper No. 3710, May 1991, and in *Industrial and Labor Relations Review*, 46 (1) (October 1992), pp. 38-54; N. Williams, "Regional Effects of the Minimum Wage on Teenage Employment," *Applied Economics*, 25 (12) (December 1993), pp. 1517-28; and D. Neumark and W. Wascher, "Employment Effects of Minimum and Subminimum Wages: Panel Data on State Minimum Wage Laws," NBER Working Paper No. 3859, October 1991, and in *Industrial and Labor Relations* Review, 46 (1) (October 1992), pp. 55-81.

8. See D. Card and A. B. Krueger, "Minimum Wages and Employment: A Case Study of the Fast-Food Industry in New Jersey and Pennsylvania," NBER Working Paper No. 4509, October 1993, and in *American Economic Review*, 84 (4) (September 1994), pp. 772-93.

9. See R. V. Burkhauser, K. A. Couch, and D. C. Wittenburg, "A Reassessment of the New Economics of the Minimum Wage Literature with Monthly Data from the Current Population Survey," *Journal of Labor Economics*, 18 (4) (October 2000), pp. 653-80; and M. Zavodny, "The Effect of the Minimum Wage on Employment and Hours." *Labour Economics*, 7 (6) (November 2000), pp. 729-50.

10. See D. Neumark and W. Wascher, "Employment Effects of Minimum and Subminimum Wages: Panel Data on State Minimum Wage Laws." See also the exchange on the evidence in this paper in D. Card, L. F. Katz, and A. B. Krueger, "Comment on David Neumark and William Wascher, 'Employment Effects of Minimum and Subminimum Wages: Panel Data on State Minimum Wage Laws'," *Industrial and Labor Relations Review*, 47 (3) (April 1994), pp. 487-96; and D. Neumark and W. Wascher, "Employment Effects of Minimum and Subminimum Wages: Reply to Card, Katz, and Krueger," NBER Working Paper No. 4570, December 1993, and in *Industrial and Labor Relations Review*, 47 (3) (April 1994), pp. 497-512.

11. D. Neumark and W. Wascher, "State-Level Estimates of Minimum Wage Effects: New Evidence and Interpretations from Disequilibrium Methods," *Journal of Human Resources*, 37 (1) (Spring 2002), pp. 35-62.

12. See D. Neumark and W. Wascher, "Minimum Wages and Employment: A Case Study of the Fast-Food Industry in New Jersey and Pennsylvania: Comment," *American Economic Review*, 90 (5) (December 2000), pp. 1362-96; and the reply in D. Card and A. B. Krueger, "Minimum Wages and Employment: A Case Study of the Fast-Food Industry in New Jersey and Pennsylvania: Reply," *American Economic Review*, 90 (5) (December 2000), pp. 1397-420.

13. V. R. Fuchs, A. B. Krueger, and J. M. Poterba, "Economists' Views About Parameters, Values, and Policies: Survey Results in Labor and Public Economics," *Journal of Economic Literature*, 36 (3) (September 1998), pp. 1387-425.

14. It is often argued that an employment elasticity as small as 0.1 or 0.2 implies that raising minimum wages raises incomes of low-wage workers, because the elasticity is much smaller (in absolute value) than 1. However, these elasticity estimates do not necessarily capture the relevant parameter, which is the elasticity of the demand for minimum wage labor with respect to the minimum. For example, these estimates ignore the possibility that the employment effects are sharpest for those at the minimum wage, pay no regard to possible hours effects, and use the legislated minimum wage change-rather than the typically smaller actual change-in the dominator. In the other direction, this calculation also ignores possible wage increases for workers above the minimum wage.

15. D. Neumark, M. Schweitzer, and W. Wascher, "Minimum Wage Effects Throughout the Wage Distribution," NBER Working Paper No. 7519, February 2000.

16. For minimum wage workers, the hours elasticities are in the range of 0.2 to 0.25, the employment elasticities in the range of 0.12 to 0.17, and the earned income elasticity is approximately -0.6. Whatever one makes of the precise estimates, clearly the evidence does not support the conclusion that minimum wage increases raise the earnings of minimum wage workers.

17. R.V. Burkhauser, K. A. Couch, and D. C. Wittenburg, 1996, "'Who Gets What' from Minimum Wage Hikes: A Re-Estimation of Card and Krueger's Distributional Analysis in Myth and Measurement: The New Economics of the Minimum Wage," *Industrial and Labor Relations Review*, 49 (3) (April 1996), pp. 547-52.

18. The estimated elasticity of the proportion poor with respect to the minimum wage is approximately 0.4. See D. Neumark, M. Schweitzer, and W. Wascher, "The Effects of Minimum Wages on the Distribution of Family Incomes: A Non-Parametric Analysis," NBER Working Paper No. 6536, April 1998. For a recent complementary parametric approach, see A. Golan, J. M. Perloff, and X. Wu, "Welfare Effects of Minimum Wage and Other Government Policies," (mimeo) University of California, Berkeley (2001).

19. See D. Neumark and W. Wascher, "Minimum Wages and Skill Acquisition: Another Look at Schooling Effects," forthcoming in *Economics of Education Review*; D. Chaplin, M. D. Turner, and A. D. Pape, "Minimum Wages and School Enrollment of Teenagers: A Look at the 1990s," forthcoming in *Economics of Education Review*; and D. Neumark and W. Wascher, "Minimum-Wage Effects on School and Work Transitions of Teenagers," *American Economic Review*, 85 (2) (May 1995), pp. 244-9.

20. D.Neumark and W. Wascher, "Minimum Wages and Training Revisited," NBER Working Paper No. 6651, July 1998, and in *Journal of Labor Economics*, 19 (3) (2001) pp. 563-95.

21. See D. Neumark, *How Living Wages Affect Low-Wage Workers and Low-Income Families*, San Francisco: Public Policy Institute of California, 2002; D. Neumark and S.Adams, "Do Living Wage Ordinances Reduce Urban Poverty?" NBER Working Paper No. 7606, March 2000, forthcoming in *Journal of Human Resources*; and D. Neumark and S. Adams, "Detecting Effects of Living Wage Laws," forthcoming in *Industrial Relations*.

22. For preliminary information on enforcement of living wage laws, see R. Sander and S. Lokey, "The Los Angeles Living Wage: The First Eighteen Months," (mimeo) UCLA and the Fair Housing Institute, Los Angeles (1998).

23. For these business assistance living wage laws, the estimated elasticity of wages with respect to living wages in the bottom decile of the wage distribution is approximately 0.1, while for contractor-only living wage laws the estimated elasticity is indistinguishable from zero. While the 0.1 elasticity may suggest a small impact, it is an average wage increase experienced by low-wage workers, whereas the actual consequence would most likely be a much larger increase concentrated on a smaller number of workers directly affected by the living wage law.

24. The estimates imply an elasticity of the proportion of poor families with respect to the living wage of about .19 This seems like a large effect, given a wage elasticity for low-wage workers of approximately 0.1. Of course no one is claiming that living wages lift a family from well below the poverty line to well above it. But living wages may help nudge a family over the poverty line, and we have to recall that these average wage effects will in fact be manifested as much larger gains concentrated on a possibly quite small number of workers and families. Thus, even coupled with some employment reductions, living wages can lift a detectable number of families above the poverty line.

25. See D. Neumark, "Living Wages: Protection For or Protection From Low-Wage Workers?" NBER Working Paper No. 8393.

3

Minimum Wage Has No Effect on Poverty and Reduces Jobs

James Sherk

James Sherk is a research fellow in labor economics at The Heritage Foundation.

Proponents of minimum wage increases insist that higher wages will help the economy across the board, but there are studies that argue to contrary, showing that minimum wage has been ineffective at lifting low-income families out of poverty and claiming that higher minimum wages reduce overall employment and displace disadvantaged workers. A fascinating case study of American Samoa in particular shows that increases in the minimum wage led to a 14 percent decrease in overall employment. What does that mean for the wage gap issue?

Chairman Harkin, Ranking Member Alexander, and Members of the HELP Committee, thank you for inviting me to testify this afternoon. My name is James Sherk. I am a Senior Policy Analyst in Labor Economics at The Heritage Foundation. The views I express in this testimony are my own, and should not be construed as representing any official position of The Heritage Foundation.

Supporters of the minimum wage intend it to lift low-income families out of poverty. Unfortunately, despite these good intentions, the minimum wage has proved ineffective at doing so. Indeed,

"What is Minimum Wage: Its History and Effects on the Economy," by James Sherk, The Heritage Foundation, June 26, 2013. Reprinted by Permission.

it often holds back many of the workers its proponents want to help. Higher minimum wages both reduce overall employment and encourage relatively affluent workers to enter the labor force. Minimum wage increases often lead to employers replacing disadvantaged adults who need a job with suburban teenagers who do not.

This can have long-term consequences. Minimum wage positions are typically learning wage positions—they enable workers to gain the skills necessary to become more productive on the job. As workers become more productive they command higher pay and move up their career ladder. Two-thirds of minimum wage workers earn a raise within a year. Raising the minimum wage makes such entry-level positions less available, in effect sawing off the bottom rung of many workers' career ladders. This hurts these workers' career prospects.

Even if minimum wage workers do not lose their job, the overlapping and uncoordinated design of U.S. welfare programs prevents those in need from benefitting from higher wages. As their income rises they lose federal tax credits and assistance. These benefit losses offset most of the wage increase. A single mother with one child faces an effective marginal tax rate of 91 percent when her pay rises from $7.25 to $10.10 an hour. Studies also find higher minimum wages do not reduce poverty rates. Despite the best of intentions, the minimum wage has proved an ineffective—and often counterproductive—policy in the war on poverty.

Congress could do more to help low-income families by restructuring and coordinating welfare programs and their associated phase-out rates. No one in America—and especially not low-income workers—should face tax rates in excess of 50 percent.

History of the Minimum Wage

Congress instituted the minimum wage in 1938 as part of the Fair Labor Standards Act (FLSA). The first minimum wage stood at 25 cents an hour. The last minimum wage increase occurred in 2007, when Congress raised the rate in steps from $5.15 an hour that year to $7.25 an hour in July 2009. The District of Columbia and 19 states have also established local minimum wages higher than the federal rate. The highest state minimum wage in the country occurs in Washington State at $9.19 an hour. The average minimum wage in the U.S.—including higher state rates—currently stands at $7.57 an hour.[1]

Over the past 65 years the minimum wage has varied considerably in inflation-adjusted buying power. It has averaged $6.60 an hour in purchasing power in 2013 dollars. But it has ranged from a low of $3.09 an hour in late 1948 to a high of $8.67 an hour in 1968.[2] Today's minimum wage buys somewhat more than the minimum wage has historically, although it remains over a dollar an hour below its historical high.[3]

Current Minimum Wage Comparison to Historical Average

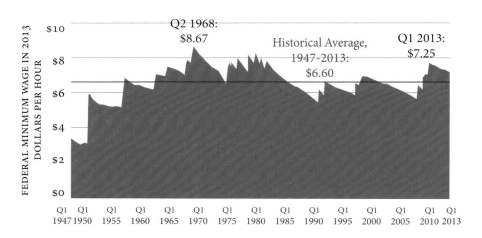

SOURCE: U.S. Department of Labor, Wage and Hour Division

Congress typically raises the minimum wage only during times of healthy economic growth and low unemployment. In 1990, Congress enacted a minimum wage hike that took effect on April 1 of that year, when unemployment stood at 5.4 percent. Congress voted to raise the minimum wage again in August 1996—when unemployment stood at 5.1 percent. The next vote to raise the minimum wage occurred in May 2007, when unemployment stood at 4.4 percent.[4] Congress has not voted to raise the minimum wage when unemployment stood above 7.5 percent since the Great Depression ended.[5]

Who Earns the Minimum Wage?

Stereotypes of minimum wage earners range from teenagers holding summer jobs to single mothers struggling to support their family. Bureau of Labor Statistics (BLS) data sheds light on who actually makes the minimum wage.

Relatively few Americans do so. In 2011 and 2012, 3.7 million Americans reported earning $7.25 or less per hour—just 2.9 percent of all workers in the United States.[6][7][8] Those who do work in minimum-wage jobs fall into two distinct categories: young workers, usually in school, and older workers who have left school. Most minimum-wage earners fall into the first category; just over half are between the ages of 16 and 24.[9] The rest are 25 or older. Table 1 shows the characteristics of minimum wage workers overall, and broken down by age groups.

Minimum-wage workers under 25 are typically not their family's sole breadwinners. Rather, they tend to live in middle-class households that do not rely on their earnings—their average family income exceeds $65,000 a year. Generally, they have not finished their schooling and are working part-time jobs. Over three-fifths of them (62 percent) are currently enrolled in school.[10] Only 22 percent live at or below the poverty line, while two-thirds live in families with incomes exceeding 150 percent of the poverty line. These workers represent the largest group that would benefit directly from a higher minimum wage, provided they kept or could find a job.

Adults who earn the minimum wage are less likely to live in middle- and upper-income families. Nonetheless, three-fourths of older workers earning the minimum wage live above the poverty line. They have an average family income of $42,500 a year, well

Characteristics of Minimum-Wage Workers

	ALL EMPLOYEES	MINIMUM WAGE EARNERS		
		ALL	AGE 16-24	AGE 25+
FEMALE	48%	63%	60%	67%
WHITE	80%	78%	80%	76%
BLACK	13%	15%	14%	17%
ASIAN	4%	3%	2%	4%
MARRIED	47%	23%	5%	41%
WAGE AND INCOME CHARACTERISTICS				
WORKING PART TIME	19%	67%	79%	54%
AVERAGE FAMILY INCOME	$79,534	$53,113	$65,896	$42,462
AT OR BELOW POVERTY LINE	6%	23%	22%	24%
ABOVE 150% OF THE POVERTY LINE	89%	65%	68%	62%
EDUCATIONAL ATTAINMENT				
LESS THAN HIGH SCHOOL	8%	28%	34%	22%
HIGH SCHOOL GRADUATE	27%	30%	23%	37%
SOME COLLEGE	28%	34%	40%	29%
BACHELOR'S DEGREE	23%	6%	3%	10%
GRADUATE DEGREE	13%	1%	0%	2%

SOURCE: Heritage Foundation calculations based on data from U.S. Census Bureau, Current Population Survey, 2011 and 2012 monthly surveys.

above the poverty line of $23,050 per year for a family of four. Most (54 percent) of them choose to work part time, and two-fifths are married.

Many advocates of raising the minimum wage argue it will help low-income single parents surviving on it as their only source of income. Minimum-wage workers, however, do not fit this stereotype. Just 4 percent of minimum-wage workers are single parents working full time, compared to 5.6 percent of all U.S. workers.[11] Minimum-wage earners are actually less likely to be single parents working full time than the average American worker.

Though some minimum-wage workers do struggle with poverty, they are not representative of the typical worker in minimum-wage jobs. The data simply does not support the stereotype of minimum-wage workers living on the edge of destitution.

Learning Wage Positions

Most minimum wage jobs are entry-level positions filled by workers with limited education and experience. As Table 1 shows, almost three-fifths of minimum wage workers have no more than a high school education. They work for the minimum wage because they currently lack the productivity to command higher pay.

Minimum-wage jobs give these workers experience and teach them essential job skills. Sometimes these skills are unique to an individual job, such as how to operate a particular piece of equipment. More often they pertain to general employability: the discipline of waking up early to go to work each day, learning how to interact with customers and coworkers, how to accept direction from a boss. These skills are essential to getting ahead in the workplace, but difficult to learn without actual on-the-job experience.

Once workers gain these skills they become more productive, and most quickly earn raises. Over two-thirds of workers starting out at the minimum wage earn more than that a year later.[12] Minimum-wage jobs are learning wage jobs—they teach inexperienced employees skills that make them more productive. They are the first step on many workers' career ladders.

While very few Americans currently work for the minimum wage, a substantial number once did so. Over half of American started their careers making within one dollar of the minimum wage.[13] Most quickly get promoted as their productivity increases.

Workers have a say in how quickly they get promoted. Most minimum-wage earners work part time, and many are students and young adults who desire this flexibility. But minimum-wage workers who choose to work longer hours gain more skills and experience than those who work part time and, as expected, earn larger raises. A typical minimum-wage employee who works 35 hours or more a week is 13 percentage points more likely to be promoted within a year than is a minimum-wage worker putting in fewer than 10 hours per week.[14]

The notion that workers are trapped earning $7.25 an hour for much of their working lives is mistaken and ignores the primary value of minimum-wage jobs. Their importance lies not so much in the low wages they pay in the present, but in making workers more productive so they can command higher pay in the future.

Labor Demand Falls as Prices Increase

One of the central premises of economics is that "demand curves slope downwards"—when prices rise people buy less of a good or service. When gasoline becomes more expensive Americans drive less, and when it becomes less costly Americans drive more. The same applies to business owners. When the price of goods or services they use in production rises, they buy less of them. This includes labor costs—when wages rise employers hire fewer workers. Economists estimate the long-run elasticity of labor demand in the U.S. economy at around –0.3.[15] In other words, a ten percent increase in labor costs causes employers to cut their workforce by three percent. Higher compensation costs without corresponding increases in productivity cause employers to hire fewer workers.

This finding applies to employers of both highly skilled and unskilled workers.[16] Employers will not pay a worker more than their productive value to a firm. Businesses that do so quickly go out of businesses.

American Samoa

The recent experience of American Samoa dramatically illustrates how wage increases reduce employment. The tiny Pacific island chain has been an American territory for over a century. However, American Samoans have a largely separate economy and considerably lower incomes than residents of the continental United States: the average Samoan worker made $12,000 in 2009.[17] The tuna canning industry makes up a significant portion of their private sector.

Until recently American Samoa had a different minimum wage schedule than the continental United States. A committee within the Department of Labor set Samoan wage minimums according to local economic conditions. In January 2007 the minimum wage in the canning industry stood at $3.26 an hour. Unfortunately for American Samoa, Congress applied the 2007 federal minimum wage increase to the territory. The legislation aligned the Samoan minimum wage with the U.S. rate of $7.25 an hour in 50 cent annual increments.[18]

Almost every hourly worker in the tuna canning industry makes less than $7.25 an hour.[19] At that level the minimum wage would cover 80 percent of the islands' hourly workers.[20] This would be the economic equivalent of raising the minimum wage to $20.00 an hour in the continental U.S.[21]

By May 2009 the third scheduled minimum wage increase in Samoa took effect, rising to $4.76 an hour and covering 69 percent of canning workers. This did not increase purchasing power, stimulate demand, and raise living standards, as many minimum wage proponents theorize. Instead StarKist—one of the two canneries then located in Samoa—laid off workers, cut hours and benefits, and froze hiring.[22] The other cannery—Chicken of the Sea—shut down entirely in September 2009.[23]

The Government Accountability Office reports that between 2006 and 2009 overall employment in American Samoa fell 14 percent and inflation-adjusted wages fell 11 percent. Employment in the tuna canning industry fell 55 percent.[24] The

GAO attributed much of these economic losses to the minimum wage hike.

The Democratic Governor of American Samoa, Togiola Tulafona, harshly criticized this GAO report for understating the damage done by the minimum wage hike. Testifying before Congress Gov. Tulafona objected that "this GAO report does not adequately, succinctly or clearly convey the magnitude of the worsening economic disaster in American Samoa that has resulted primarily from the imposition of the 2007 US minimum wage mandate."[25] Gov. Tulafona pointed out that American Samoa's unemployment rate jumped from 5 percent before the last minimum wage hike to over 35 percent in 2009.[26] He begged Congress to stop increasing the islands' minimum wage:

"We are watching our economy burn down. We know what to do to stop it. We need to bring the aggressive wage costs decreed by the Federal Government under control. But we are ordered not to interfere…Our job market is being torched. Our businesses are being depressed. Our hope for growth has been driven away… Our question is this: How much does our government expect us to suffer, until we have to stand up for our survival?"[27]

Samoan employers responded to higher labor costs the way economic theory predicts: by hiring fewer workers. Congress hurt the very workers it intended to help. Fortunately, Congress heeded the Governor's plea and suspended the future scheduled minimum wage increases.

Minimum Wage Employment Effects

Virtually no economist doubts that raising the minimum wage to $20.00 an hour in the mainland U.S. would have similar consequences. Economists only debate the consequences of small minimum wage increases.

In part this is because, at current rates, the minimum wage affects very few workers, so it has relatively small effects on the overall economy. Even groups considered highly affected by the minimum wage have few minimum-wage workers overall.

Just one-fifth of teenagers and restaurant employees work for the federal minimum wage.[28] Raising the minimum wage by $1.00 an hour—as many states have done—has little effect on most workers, even most teenagers. Consequently, a moderate increase in the minimum wage will have only small effects on the U.S. economy. It affects too few workers to have a larger impact. A law eliminating a tenth of minimum-wage jobs would raise overall unemployment by less than 0.3 percentage point.[29] Congress should not conflate small effects with no effect. The minimum wage does hurt the prospects of the relatively small number of workers it covers.

Until the mid-1990s, labor economists had a consensus that a 10 percent increase in the minimum wage reduced employment of impacted groups (like teenagers) by about 2 percent.[30] Research by David Card of the University of California-Berkeley challenged this conclusion.[31] His research, focusing on case studies of states that raised the minimum wage and states that did not, concluded the minimum wage had no adverse effect on employment. This spurred an explosion of research on the topic. This research coincided with a significant number of states raising their minimum wages above the federal level in the 1990s and 2000s. These state increases created far more case studies for economists to analyze and permitted panel studies utilizing variation in minimum wage rates across all U.S. states.

Two-thirds of the studies in this "new minimum wage research" utilizing state variation in minimum wages came to the same conclusion that previous economists had: higher minimum wages reduce the employment of less-skilled workers.[32] Among the most methodologically rigorous studies, 85 percent came to this conclusion.

A recent line of papers by Michael Reich, Arindrajit Dube, and Sylvia Allegretto contest these findings.[33] They argue that states that raised their minimum wage above the federal level (typically in the Northeast and West Coast) have slower underlying employment growth than states that did not raise their minimum wage (typically in the South and Mountain West). They contend that studies finding negative employment effects conflate these pre-existing trends with the effects of higher minimum wages. They find that once researchers control for state or regional trends the negative relationship goes away. They then compared counties that border each other across a state line and concluded higher minimum wages have negligible employment effects on teenagers and restaurant employees.

David Neumark of the University of California–Irvine and William Wascher of the Federal Reserve Board strongly dispute this critique.[34] They show that the evidence for pre-existing trends biasing previous studies is weak. They demonstrate that it takes very specific controls to make the relationship between the minimum wage and job losses disappear. Using more general specifications favored by economists produces the standard conclusion that minimum wage increases cost jobs.

Neumark and Wascher also argue that the many counties compared across state borders have very different economic climates. For example, Dube et al. compare urban Leon County in Florida (the home county of Tallahassee) with its population of 275,000 to rural Grady County, Georgia—population 25,000. Neumark and Wascher used statistical tests to analyze how closely the labor markets of these cross-border counties resemble each other. They find that among reasonable candidates for comparison, the cross-border counties "appear no better than a random draw."[35]

They conclude that economists should look at data from all states, not just cross-border comparisons, and use standard specifications to control for pre-existing trends. Doing so produces the usual finding that minimum wage increases cost jobs. Raising the price of unskilled labor causes employers to hire fewer unskilled workers.

Crowding Out Disadvantaged Workers

The minimum wage especially hurts disadvantaged workers' job prospects. Higher minimum wages encourage employers to replace less-skilled workers with more productive employees. Given the choice between hiring an unskilled worker for $10.10 an hour and a worker with more experience for the same rate, companies will always choose the more experienced and productive employee.

Higher minimum wages also make working in such jobs more attractive, drawing greater numbers of workers with outside sources of income into the labor market. Many suburban teenagers and college students enter the labor market when the minimum wage rises. As they apply for job openings they crowd out urban teenagers and disadvantaged adults who would have sought the jobs at the previous wages. Overall, the minimum wage reduces disadvantaged workers' employment much more than it reduces overall employment. It causes the very workers minimum wage advocates most want to help to have the greatest difficulty finding jobs.

Empirical research consistently bears this out. One recent study examined administrative data from a large retail chain.[36] When the minimum wage rose, the chain slightly reduced overall employment. Surprisingly, however, teenage employment rose in several stores. These teen employment gains came at the expense of larger job losses among adults. The composition of teenage employment also changed, with more teens coming from wealthier neighborhoods and fewer from low-income neighborhoods. The higher wages prompted many suburban teenagers to apply for work. They crowded many low-income adults and youth out of jobs.

Another study examined how teenage employment and school enrollment changed after states raised their minimum wage.[37] It found that when states raised their minimum wage, younger teens and those who had dropped out of school were more likely to become unemployed. At the same time, higher-skill teenagers were more likely get jobs. When they have to pay higher wages, businesses hire higher-skill workers, freezing the least productive workers out of the job market.

Even studies that find the minimum wage has negligible overall employment effects find it decreases the employment of disadvantaged workers. Kevin Lang and Shulamit Kahn of Boston University examined how restaurant employment changed after minimum wage hikes in the late 1980s and early 1990s.[38] They found no evidence that the minimum wage reduced total restaurant employment, but they did find that it dramatically changed the mix of workers that restaurants hired. Teenage and student employment rose, while adult employment dropped.

A higher minimum wage is great news for a high school student working part time to buy an iPhone. It hurts lower-skill adult workers who need work to support themselves and perhaps their families. Making entry-level jobs less available makes it harder for them to gain the skills and experience necessary to advance to better paying jobs. The minimum wage effectively saws off the first rung on their career ladder.

Little Benefit to Families in Poverty

The minimum wage raises the pay of many workers at the cost of some jobs. A lot of advocates for minimum wage increases consider this a good trade-off. They argue that the gains for the workers who benefit far outweigh the costs to those who lose out. For example, raising the minimum wage by 40 percent—from $7.25 an hour to $10.10 an hour—would cost roughly 8 percent of heavily affected worker groups their jobs (although losses would be larger among the most disadvantaged workers).[39] At first glance this may seem like a good deal.

However, this analysis ignores the way American tax and welfare programs claw back wage gains made by low-income workers. Congress has created many overlapping means-tested benefit programs: the supplemental nutrition assistance program (SNAP, formerly called food stamps), temporary assistance for needy families (TANF), the Earned Income Tax Credit (EITC), child-care subsidies, housing vouchers, and Women, Infants, and Children (WIC) benefits. The government also provides extensive in-kind health care benefits: Medicaid, SCHIP, and the soon to be operating health care exchange subsidies.

These benefits phase out at different rates as income rises. Earning an additional dollar of income reduces SNAP benefits by 24 cents. Workers in the EITC phase-out range lose 21 cents for each additional dollar they earn. Housing vouchers phase out at a 30 percent rate. Low-income workers must also pay payroll (15 percent) and income taxes (10-15 percent) on each additional dollar of income. Medicaid operates with a cliff: when workers' incomes exceed a certain threshold, they lose all benefits.

Congress did not coordinate these benefit phase-outs across programs. Consequently low-income workers can face very high effective tax rates as they lose benefits from multiple programs. Consider workers both losing SNAP benefits and landing in the EITC phase out range. For each additional dollar they earn they pay 15 cents in additional payroll taxes, 15 cents in income taxes, an average of 5 cents in state income taxes, as well as losing 21 cents of their EITC benefit and forgoing 24 cents of SNAP benefits—an effective marginal tax rate of 80 percent. Each extra dollar earned increases their net income by only 20 cents. Not even millionaires pay such high tax rates.

The Congressional Budget Office studied this issue in a report released last year.[40] It found that a single parent with one child earning between $15,000 to $25,000 experiences almost no financial benefit from working additional hours or getting a raise.[41] What they gain in market income they lose in reduced benefits, leaving them no better off.

The academic literature concludes that low-income families financially benefit when the head of the household enters the labor force and takes a job that pays near the poverty level. However, additional hours of work—or higher wages—beyond that generally produce little additional net benefit until earnings exceed 150 to 200 percent of the poverty level.[42]

Unfortunately, minimum-wage workers with incomes below the poverty level fall into this earnings dead zone. A childless adult working full time for the minimum wage earns $15,080 a year, above the poverty level for one person ($11,490). That adult (or a teenager) qualifies for relatively few federal benefits. But a single parent working the same job would fall below the poverty level for either one ($15,510) or two ($19,530) children. That single parent qualifies for many means-tested federal benefits. If the federal minimum wage rose to $10.10 an hour ($21,008 a year for a full-time job) benefit reductions would claw back the majority of his or her raise.

[...]

Nationwide, the average single parent with one child who participates in all programs for which they are eligible faces an effective marginal tax rate of 91 percent. The same parent with two children faces an effective tax rate of 79 percent. In some states the raise would actually financially hurt families.

Consider a Patty Jones, a hypothetical single mother in Des Moines, Iowa, who gets an offer for a job at minimum wage.[43] If she goes from not working to working full time, her monthly income rises from $1,146 to $1,838. However, if she gets a raise to $10.10 an hour, her monthly income falls to $1,574. She loses over $260. While her market income rises by $494, she loses $71 in EITC refunds, pays $37 more in payroll taxes and $45 more in state income taxes. She also loses $88 in food stamp benefits and $528 in child-care subsidies. Patty would be better off without the raise.

This system makes it very difficult to lift families out of poverty by raising the minimum wage. Higher minimum wages make it more difficult for disadvantaged adults to find jobs. This hurts their finances. However, for those living below the poverty line who keep their job, the raise provides little net benefit. Much or all of what they gain in higher pay gets clawed back as reduced benefits.

College students and teenagers with jobs do benefit from a higher minimum wage; they have few government benefits to lose. But Congress does not raise the minimum wage to help teenagers buy jeans or iPhones. It does so to help families struggling below the poverty line. Current law makes it almost impossible to achieve that goal.

No Effect on Poverty

Economic research further shows that raising the minimum wage does not reduce poverty.[44] Economists have studied changes in aggregate state poverty rates when states raise their minimum wage. They have also examined micro-data on individual families' finances when the minimum wage changes. A study finds minimum wages reduce poverty.[45] One other study finds the opposite result.[46] But the overwhelming balance of recent research finds no effect of the minimum wage on poverty.[47] Even David Card, a researcher celebrated by minimum wage advocates, comes to this conclusion.[48]

This should come as little surprise. Besides reducing job opportunities and the perverse structure of the welfare state, very few poor families have any minimum wage workers. Only 11 percent of the workers who would gain from raising the minimum wage to $9.50 an hour live at or below the poverty line.[49]

In fact, very few poor families have any full-time workers at all. Only 9 percent of adults living below the poverty line work full time year round. One quarter work part time. Two-thirds of adults living below the poverty line do not work at all.[50] Raising the minimum wage hurts their job prospects but does nothing to increase their earnings—they have none.

If Congress wants to reduce poverty it should focus on restructuring the welfare state to remove the current disincentives to work. For too many low-income families additional work does not pay. Few Americans at any income level would work longer hours when faced with a tax rate exceeding 50 percent.

Footnotes

1. Heritage Foundation calculations using data on state minimum wage rates from the Department of Labor, Wage and Hour Division. The figure is a weighted average, where the weights are each state's respective share of hourly employees in the U.S.
2. Source: Heritage Foundation calculations using data from the Department of Labor, Wage and Hour Division. Inflation adjusted using the Personal Consumption Expenditures (PCE) price index.
3. Analysis inflation adjusting historical minimum wage rates with the Consumer Price Index (CPI) will report higher real rates. The CPI estimates higher inflation than the PCE index and other chained measures of inflation do. This results in a larger upwards to historical rates to account for inflation. Using the CPI the minimum wage stood at $10.60 an hour in 1968. However, economists widely agree that the Laspreyes fixed-basket methodology the CPI utilizes produces less accurate estimates than a chained-index methodology. Consequently this paper uses the PCE index to adjust for past inflation. See for example Clinton McCully, Brian Moyer, and Kenneth Stewart, "A Reconciliation between the Consumer Price Index and the Personal Consumption Expenditures Price Index," *Bureau of Economic Analysis Papers*, September 2007.
4. Department of Labor, Bureau of Labor Statistics, "The Employment Situation," April 1990, August 1996, May 2007.
5. Although the economy has slipped into recessions after minimum wage increases (such as in 2007), these contractions were not expected when Congress voted.
6. Heritage Foundation analysis of data from the Current Population Survey (CPS). The Census Bureau and Bureau of Labor Statistics jointly conduct the CPS. All numbers, except average family income and poverty status, come from analysis of the 2011 and 2012 Merged Outgoing Rotation Group (MORG) file of the CPS. Minimum-wage earners were defined as hourly employees paid $7.25 an hour or less. Poverty and family income statistics come from the March supplement to the 2011 and 2012 CPS data. Data available for download at http://thedataweb.rm.census.gov/ftp/cps_ftp.html and https://cps.ipums.org/cps/
7. The 2.9 percent figure includes both salaried and hourly employees. Approximately 5 percent of hourly employees get paid the federal minimum wage.
8. These numbers include workers who also earn tip income. Many of those earning less than the minimum wage work in restaurants and make more than the minimum wage after taking tips into account.
9. 50.5 percent of minimum wage earners are between the ages of 16 and 24.
10. Heritage Foundation calculations using the 2011 and 2012 Current Population Survey. The months of June, July, and August were excluded to avoid conflating summer breaks with non-enrollment.
11. Heritage Foundation analysis of data from the Current Population Survey (CPS). A single parent is defined as someone who reports that he or she has one or more of his or her own children present in the household and who is widowed, divorced, separated, or never married. Full-time employees are classified as those working 35 or more hours a week.
12. David Macpherson and William Even, "Wage Growth Among Minimum Wage Workers," Employment Policies Institute, June 2004, p. 3-5, at www.epionline.org/studies/macpherson_06-2004.pdf.
13. William Carrington and Bruce Fallick, "Do Some Workers Have Minimum Wage Careers," *Monthly Labor Review*, May 2001, pp. 17-27, Table 2
14. Macpherson and Even, "Wage Growth Among Minimum Wage Workers," pp. 8-11.

15. Daniel S. Hamermesh, *Labor Demand* (Princeton, N.J.: Princeton University Press, 1993).

16. Although studies typically find workers with greater skills have a smaller elasticity of demand.

17. Government Accountability Office, *American Samoa and the Commonwealth of the Northern Mariana Islands: Employment, Earnings, and Status of Key Industries Since Minimum Wage Increases Began*, Report No. GAO-11-427, June 2011, Figure 11.

18. *Ibid.*, Table 4.

19. Government Accountability Office, *American Samoa and the Commonwealth of the Northern Mariana Islands,* p. 63.

20. U.S. Department of Labor, *Impact of Increased Minimum Wages on the Economies of American Samoa and the Commonwealth of the Northern Mariana Islands*, January 2008.

21. Heritage Foundation calculations using data from the Outgoing Rotation Groups of the 2012 monthly current population survey. $20.00 an hour is the 80th percentile for workers paid hourly wages.

22. Government Accountability Office, *American Samoa and the Commonwealth of the Northern Mariana Islands* p. 63.

23. *Ibid.*, p. 40.

24. *Ibid.*, Table 2.

25. Testimony of American Samoa Governor Togiola Tulafona before the Subcommittee on Fisheries, Wildlife, Oceans and Insular Affairs of the Committee on Natural Resources, U.S. House of Representatives, September 23, 2011. Opening statement available online at http://americansamoa.gov/index.php/news-bottom/30-gov-togiola-tells-u-s-congress-minimum-wage-increase-will-destroy-as-economy

26. *Ibid.*, Written Testimony, Table 3.

27. *Ibid.*, opening statement.

28. Department of Labor, Bureau of Labor Statistics, "Characteristics of Minimum Wage Workers—2012," Tables 1 and 4, athttp://www.bls.gov/cps/minwage2012tbls.htm.

29. The increase in unemployed would probably be less—many of these workers, especially teenagers and college students, would probably drop out of the labor market altogether and no longer count as unemployed.

30. Charles Brown, Curtis Gilroy, and Andrew Kohen, "The Effect of the Minimum Wage on Employment and Unemployment," *Journal of EconomicLiterature* Vol. 20, No. 2 (June 1982), pp. 487–528.

31. David Card and Alan Krueger. "Minimum Wages and Employment: A Case Study of Fast-Food Industry in New Jersey and Pennsylvania," *American Economic Review*, Vol. 48, No. 4 (1994), pp. 772-793.

32. David Neumark and William Wascher, *Minimum Wages* (Cambridge, MA: The MIT Press, 2008).

33. See for example Sylvia Allegretto, Arindrajit Dube, and Michael Reich, "Spatial Heterogeneity and Minimum Wages: Employment Estimates for Teens Using Cross-State Commuting Zones," Berkeley, CA: Institute for Research on Labor and Employment, 2009; Sylvia Allegretto, Arindrajit Dube, and Michael Reich, "Do Minimum Wages Really Reduce Teen Employment? Accounting for Heterogeneity and Selectivity in State Panel Data," *Industrial Relations*, Vol. 50, No. 2, pp. 205-240; Arindrajit Dube, T. William Lester, and Michael Reich, "Minimum Wage Effects Across State Borders: Estimates Using Contiguous Counties," *Review of Economics and Statistics*, Vol. 92, No. 4 (2010), pp. 945-964.

34. David Neumark, Ian Salas, and William Wascher, "Revisiting the Minimum Wage-Employment Debate: Throwing Out the Baby with the Bathwater?" National Bureau

of Economic Research Working Paper No. 18681 (2013), http://www.nber.org/papers/w18681.

35. *Ibid.*, pp. 27-28.

36. Laura Giuliano, "Minimum Wage Effects on Employment, Substitution, and the Teenage Labor Supply: Evidence from Personnel Data," *The Journal of Labor Economics*, Vol. 31, No. 1 (January 2013), pp. 155-194.

37. David Neumark and William Wascher. "The Effects of Minimum Wages on Teenage Employment and Enrollment: Evidence from Matched CPS Surveys," in Solomon Polchek, ed. *Research in Labor Economics*, Vol. 15 (Greenwich, Conn.: JAI Press, 1996).

38. Kevin Lang and Shulamit Kahn, "The Effect of Minimum-Wage Laws on the Distribution of Employment: Theory and Evidence,"*Journal of Public Economics*, Vol. 69, No. 1 (July 1998), pp. 67-82.

39. This assumes an employment elasticity of –0.2.

40. Congressional Budget Office, "Effective Marginal Tax Rates for Low—and Moderate-Income Workers," November 2012,http://www.cbo.gov/sites/default/files/cbofiles/attachments/11-15-2012-MarginalTaxRates.pdf.

41. *Ibid.*, Summary Figure 1.

42. Elaine Maag, C. Eugene Steuerle, Ritadhi Chakravarti, and Caleb Quakenbush, "How Marginal Tax Rates Affect Families at Various Levels of Poverty," *National Tax Journal*, Vol. 65, No. 4 (December 2012), pp 759-782.

43. All assumptions are the same as for a single parent with one child as explained in the footnotes of Table 2.

44. Note that this does not follow directly from the preceding section. Poverty calculations exclude non-cash benefits like Medicaid, SNAP, and housing vouchers.

45. John Addison and McKinley L. Blackburn, "Minimum Wages and Poverty, *Industrial and Labor Relations Review* Vol. 52, No. 3 (1999), pp. 393–409.

46. David Neumark, Mark Schweitzer, and William Wascher, "The Effects of Minimum Wages on the Distribution of Family Incomes: A Non-Parametric Analysis," *Journal of Human Resources* Vol. 40, No. 4 (2005), pp.867–94.

47. Richard V. Burkhauser and Joseph J. Sabia, "Minimum Wages and Poverty: Will a \$9.50 Federal Minimum Wage Really Help the Working Poor?" *Southern Economic Journal,* Vol. 77, No. 3 (January 2010); Richard Vedder and Lowell Gallaway, "Does the Minimum Wage Reduce Poverty?" Employment Policies Institute, June 2001; Jill Jenkins, "Minimum Wages: The Poor Are Not Winners," Employment Policy Foundation, January 12, 2000; Ronald B. Mincy, "Raising the Minimum Wage: Effects on Family Poverty," *Monthly Labor Review* Vol. 113, No. 7 (July 1990); Richard Burkhauser, and Joseph J. Sabia, 2007. "The Effectiveness of Minimum Wage Increases in Reducing Poverty: Past, Present, and Future," *Contemporary Economic Policy* Vol. 25, No. 2 (2007), pp. 262–281; Craig Gundersen, and James Patrick Ziliak, 2004. "Poverty and Macroeconomic Performance Across Space, Race, and Family Structure,"*Demography* Vol. 41, No. 1 (2004), pp. 61–86; David Neumark, and William Wascher. 2002. "Do Minimum Wages Fight Poverty?"*Economic Inquiry* Vol. 40, No. 3(2002) pp. 315–333.

48. David Card and Alan B. Krueger, *Myth and Measurement: The New Economics of the Minimum Wage* (Princeton, N.J.: Princeton University Press, 1995).

49. Burkhauser and Sabia, "Minimum Wages and Poverty: Will a \$9.50 Federal Minimum Wage Really Help the Working Poor?"

50. U.S. Census Bureau, Historical Poverty Tables, Table 25, "Work Experience and Poverty Status for People 16 years Old and Over: 1987-2011," http://www.census.gov/hhes/www/poverty/data/historical/hstpov25.xls

4

Raising Minimum Wage Benefits Income Inequality and Inflation

Heather Boushey

Heather Boushey is executive director and chief economist at Washington Center for Equitable Growth

Some experts say that raising the minimum wage will reduce poverty, boost productivity, and address income inequality. Furthermore, studies indicate that indexing the minimum wage to the rate of inflation will ensure that it maintains its value over time. Detractors of wage increases do not believe that the minimum wage is an important tool in fighting poverty and works in tandem with other poverty fighting measures such as the Earned Income Tax Credit.

Introduction

I would like to thank Chairman Harkin, Ranking Member Alexander, and the rest of Committee for inviting me here today to testify.

My name is Heather Boushey and I am Executive Director and Chief Economist of the Washington Center for Equitable Growth. The center is a new project devoted to understanding what grows our economy, with a particular emphasis on understanding whether and how high and rising levels of economic inequality affect economic growth in our nation.

"Understanding how raising the federal minimum wage affects income inequality and economic growth," by Heather Boushey, The Washington Center for Equitable Growth, March 12, 2014. Reprinted by Permission.

By training, I am a labor economist. I have spent my career seeking to understand the American labor market and the effects of public policy on family economic well-being and the economy more generally. It is an honor to be invited here today to discuss how a fair minimum wage will help families succeed and support broad-based income growth in our society.

The best way to fight poverty is to make sure people have jobs with decent wages that put them above the poverty line. Raising the minimum wage and ensuring that its value stays at a reasonable level over time through indexing it to the cost of living will establish a stronger first rung on the ladder to economic security. The minimum wage is the cornerstone of a set of policies, including the Earned Income Tax Credit, the Affordable Care Act, as well as some yet to be implemented nationwide, such as paid sick days and paid family and medical leave that provide the foundation for economic security for workers and their families.

There are three key conclusions from my testimony:

- Raising the minimum wage will reduce poverty. According to economic estimates, raising the minimum wage to $10.10 an hour will reduce the poverty rate for non-elderly Americans to 15.8 percent by 2016 from current 17.5 percent levels. This increase would bring about 6.8 million people out of poverty.
- Raising the minimum wage will help family breadwinners support their children. The typical minimum wage earner brings in half of their family's income. Congress should also take care to make sure that other benefits for low-wage workers provide a full package for low-wage workers and their families as families will also need help with access to affordable and quality health care, childcare, and housing, even at a higher minimum wage.
- Raising the minimum wage will have positive economic effects above and beyond lowering the poverty rate. Economic research points to the conclusion that a higher minimum wage does not cause greater unemployment,

boosts productivity, and addresses the growing problem of rising income inequality.

The rest of my testimony will focus on the facts about the minimum wage, a review of the academic literature on the impact on poverty of raising the minimum wage, and a consideration of how the minimum wage interacts with other poverty-fighting programs to help low-wage workers enter the middle class.

The State of the Minimum Wage

The federal minimum wage is currently $7.25 an hour, where it's been since July 2009. Raising the minimum wage to $10.10 would be in line with its value in the past. The minimum wage has been raised 22 times since first enacted into law in 1938, most recently in three steps between 2007 and 2009.

The Fair Minimum Wage Act of 2013 would raise the minimum wage to $10.10 in three steps, beginning three months after passage of the bill and ending two years after the first increase. The law will then index the minimum wage to the rate of inflation, ensuring that its value does not erode over time. It will also raise the minimum wage for workers who earn tips, such as food service workers, to $7.10 an hour.

The Fair Minimum Wage Act is necessary because Congress has allowed the purchasing power of the minimum wage to decline sharply in recent years, leaving too many workers toiling full-time, but not able to rise above poverty. The purchasing power of the minimum wage hit a high in 1968 and has declined by 23 percent since then in inflation-adjusted dollars, using the Bureau of Labor Statistics Consumer Price Index for all Urban Consumers Research Series.

The value of the minimum wage also has declined relative to the earnings of other wage earners. In 1968, the minimum wage was equal to just over half (53 percent) of the average wage for production and non-supervisory workers. In 2013, the minimum wage had fallen to just over a third (36 percent) of the average wage.

The Fair Minimum Wage Act sets the minimum wage at a level that will help workers and their families, be good for the economy, and is consistent with past levels of the minimum wage. If the minimum wage had been indexed to inflation starting in 1968, it would currently be $9.39. And if the minimum wage were indexed to be 50 percent of the average wage, roughly where it was in 1968, it would currently be $10.08. In inflation-adjusted dollars, by 2016 when the Fair Minimum Wage Act would be fully implemented, the minimum wage would equal about $9.45 in today's dollars, consistent with past values.

This proposed increase in the minimum wage is consistent with what the economy can provide. While the minimum wage has lost value in inflation-adjusted dollars, the overall economy has grown considerably. Between 1968 and 2013, U.S. gross domestic product grew by an inflation-adjusted 245 percent, to $15.8 trillion from $4.6 trillion while the inflation-adjusted value of the minimum wage fell by 23 percent over the same period. Or consider another means of comparison, from 1968 to 2012, the average pre-tax, pre-transfer income of the top 1 percent of households grew by 187 percent. In contrast, over the course of those same years, the share of U.S. families living under the poverty line has risen from 10 percent to 11.8 percent

Even after the increase proposed in this law, the federal minimum wage will remain a floor. Individual states and municipalities have minimum wages above the federal minimum of $7.25. Twenty-one states and the District of Columbia have higher minimum wages, with the state of Washington having the highest in the country at $9.32 per hour. We have learned from these experiences of these states that raising the minimum wage overall delivers of positive results in the fight against poverty and efforts to grow the middle class from the bottom up.

Earnings of Minimum-Wage Workers and Poverty Thresholds

Raising the minimum wage is an important anti-poverty tool, but the current minimum wage leaves too many families in poverty. Earning the current federal minimum wage, a minimum-wage earner working 40 hours a week every week of the year would earn $15,080 over the year. This amount of earnings puts a single adult just barely above poverty. But if that worker has to support any other people—such as a child—then this family would be living below the U.S. poverty threshold. The poverty line for a family with one non-elderly adult and one child was $16,057 in 2013. Therefore, a full-time minimum-wage earner with one child and no spouse would come up short by $977 each year.

Increasing the minimum wage to $10.10 by 2016, which would equal $9.45 in 2013 dollars, would boost the earnings of low-wage workers and reduce poverty. At that minimum wage, a full-time, full-year worker would earn $19,656 in 2013 dollars over the course of the year, assuming they never take a day off without pay, and be able to support two children as a single earner and be above the official poverty threshold.

Nearly a quarter (23 percent) of the workers who will benefit from the Fair Minimum Wage Act currently live in a family earning less than $20,000 in a year, just above the poverty threshold of $18,769 for a family of one adult and two children. Just under 52 percent of workers who will benefit live in a family making below $40,000 a year, which is closer to what many surveys show is what people believe is a basic standard of living for a family of four.

Economists have also explored with the likely effects of raising the minimum wage would be on poverty. Economist Arindrajit Dube, from the University of Massachusetts, Amherst, estimates that a 10 percent increase in the minimum wage would immediately decrease the poverty rate by 2.4 percent and lead to an overall reduction of 3.6 percent in the longer run. According to his estimates, which in my view are empirically sound and conform with the economics literature, the Fair Minimum Wage

Act will reduce the poverty rate for non-elderly Americans from 17.5 percent to 15.8 percent. On a longer time frame, past one year after the minimum wage increase, the rate would decrease to 15 percent, according to Dube.

In more concrete numbers, the increase would translate to around 4.6 million Americans no longer in poverty (or around 6.8 million if longer term effects are accounted for). Another way to contextualize these numbers is to note that the poverty rate for the non-elderly increased by as much as 3.4 percentage points during the Great Recession. So the proposed minimum wage increase could reverse about half of that increase. Other recent research shows that an increase in the minimum wage would reduce spending on anti-poverty programs like the Supplemental Nutrition Assistance Program.

Making Work Pay

The anti-poverty effects of the minimum wage are significant, but to pull workers and their families up and out of poverty, the minimum wage must work in tandem with income support policies. One of the most important policy interactions is with the Earned Income Tax Credit. The EITC is a refundable tax credit for low-income families that is larger for those with more dependent children. The EITC is an effective anti-poverty policy that lifts millions of Americans out of poverty. In 2012, the EITC lifted 6.5 million people out of poverty, according to the Center on Budget and Policy Priorities.

For example, the minimum wage and the EITC are designed to work together. As economists David Lee, of Princeton University and Emmanuel Saez of University of California, Berkeley, argue the optimal minimum wage should be paired with a wage subsidy, such as the EITC. This wage subsidy encourages workers to enter the labor force and the minimum wage helps ensures they receive an adequate wage to escape poverty. Looking at the data, we can see how the minimum wage and the EITC work together to pull families out of poverty. At the current minimum-wage level, a single earner (full-time, full-year) with two dependents would receive $5,372 from the EITC for a total after-federal income of $20,452 (although workers may need to pay state income taxes and will owe payroll taxes). With a minimum wage of $9.45 in 2013 dollars, a single earner would see a $4,920 boost from the EITC for a total after-federal income tax of $24,576.

A major concern with the EITC, however, is that it is a subsidy to employers who pay very low wages. According to UC-Berkeley economist Jesse Rothstein's estimates, employers capture 27 percent of the value of the EITC. The EITC induces more workers into the labor market and makes it easier for them to take lower wages, since they can get the EITC subsidy. Part of this result is because EITC-eligible workers who can afford a lower wage compete against non-eligible workers. The result is that employers get labor at a cheaper rate than they would otherwise.

One very important reason to focus on raising the minimum wage is that a higher minimum wage reduces this capture by reducing the reduction in wages caused by the increase in the supply of labor. Making more workers eligible for the EITC would also help benefit workers. The end result is both greater employment and more of the EITC subsidy going to the intended recipients, low-wage workers and their families.

Low-wage workers are eligible for a variety of benefits aimed at boosting incomes or helping them afford basics, such as housing, health care, or childcare. This is important since many basics, especially health care, childcare, and housing, are too expensive at market rates for low-income workers and their families. Childcare alone can eat up a large portion of a minimum wage workers' income. It is imperative that these programs work in tandem and that Congress—and state policymakers—consider the interaction effects of changing any of these policies. In many cases, the states set the rules for program eligibility, with some guidelines from the federal government, so engaging them in this conversation is a must.

In the mid-1990s when Congress implemented welfare reform, Congress did a very good job putting all these pieces together by looking at the benefits and income supports for low-wage workers and their families as a package. Within a short span of time, Congress implemented welfare reform, while also raising the minimum wage, expanding the EITC, expanding access to children's health through the State Children's Health Insurance Program, and expanding childcare subsidies. Only by putting a full basket of policies together will low-wage workers be able to rise out of poverty and into the middle class. The minimum wage is a core piece of this puzzle, but it is not the only piece.

Congress could do more to ensure that minimum wage workers earn a fair day's pay by making sure that when they or their child gets sick they have the right to job-protected paid sick days, as proposed in the Healthy Families Act and is now the law in a number of municipalities and the state of Connecticut. Further, most minimum wage workers do not have the right to vacation time or paid family and medical leave, making it difficult for them to care for their families while working full-time.

Economic Effects of Raising the Minimum Wage

Raising the minimum wage is not only an effective anti-poverty tool but also a proven way to boost our economy more generally. The economics evidence shows that raising the minimum wage does not lead to higher unemployment overall but rather boosts productivity and addresses a growing issue in our economy of rising inequality.

Careful studies of the economics literature find that increases in the minimum wage have little to no effect on employment. Economists David Card, of the University of California, Berkeley, and Alan Krueger, of Princeton University, looked at the effects of a minimum wage hike in New Jersey by comparing fast food restaurant employment in the state to fast food employment in Pennsylvania which did not increase its minimum wage. Card and Krueger found that the increase in the minimum wage did not reduce employment. Their approach has been generalized in later research. Research by Arindrajit Dube, T. William Lester of the University of North Carolina—Chapel Hill, and Michael Reich of the University of California, Berkeley looked at all of the bordering counties that have different minimum wages between 1990 and 2006. They too found that minimum wage did not have a significant effect on employment.

One reason that employment has not been shown to fall due to raising the minimum wage is because higher wages can make workers more productive and therefore more valuable to their employer. Economists call this the "efficiency wages" theory. There is an extensive literature on efficiency wage theory, with notable contributions Nobel Laureates Joseph Stiglitz and George Akerlof, which suggest that paying more than the market-clearing wage can make firms more productive.

As the White House pointed out last week, higher wages can "boost productivity, increase morale, reduce costs, and improve efficiency." Here are just two academic studies that prove these points. John Schmitt, a Senior Economist at the Center for Economic and Policy Research, finds empirical economics research suggesting efficiency gains. And in a 2011 study, Georgia State University economists Barry Hirsch and Bruce Kaufman, along with Tetyana Zelenska from Innovations for Poverty Action, examined the effect of a federal increase in the minimum wage on 81 restaurants in Georgia and Alabama. In their survey, managers reported that they could identify possible non-wage savings and productivity improvements in response to the minimum-wage regulations. It is possible that lower costs stemming from these changes could outweigh the costs of paying a higher minimum wage.

In addition, it's possible that a higher minimum wage could make staying in one's job more attractive and thus reduce turnover costs. A 2013 working paper by UMass-Amherst economist Arindrajit Dube, University of North Carolina, Chapel Hill economist William Lester, and UC-Berkeley economist Michael Reich finds that a higher minimum wage leads to fewer so called "hires and separations," or worker turnover. Other empirical studies suggesting that a higher minimum wage—or a "living wage" covering basic needs—can reduce labor turnover include studies of workers in San Francisco (including airport and homecare workers) and Los Angeles. Lower turnover costs could potentially allow businesses to overcome the increased cost of paying a higher wage.

Finally, the level of the minimum wage has a considerable effect on the distribution of wages in the United States. As mentioned above, the minimum wage used to be much closer to the average wage. But since 1968, the average wage grew as the purchasing power of the minimum wage declined by 23 percent. At the same time, the distance between wage earner at the 10th percentile and median wage earner, or the earner at the 50th percentile, grew by 18 percent from 1979 to 2009.

Economists have found that the declining inflation-adjusted value of the minimum wage had a considerable effect on wage inequality for those workers in the bottom half of the wage distribution. A 1996 paper by economists John DiNardo, of the University of Michigan, Nicole Fortin, of the University of British Columbia, and Thomas Lemieux, also of the University of British Columbia, found that the decrease in the minimum wage from 1979 to 1988 had a considerable effect on the wage distribution. They found the decline over that time could explain up to 25 percent of the change in the standard deviation in the logarithm of male wages and up to 30 percent for female wages. In plain English, this means the decline in the minimum wage explained up to a fourth of increasing wage inequality for men and up to three-tenths of increase wage inequality for women.

In more recent work, MIT economist David Autor, London School of Economics economist Alan Manning, and Federal Reserve Board economist Christopher Smith find that about 75 percent of the increase in low-end inequality from 1979 to 1991 is due to the decline in the value of the minimum wage, but the decline only explains 45 percent of the increase from 1979 to 2009.

While the literature has not come to an agreement on the exact size of the effect, the decline of the minimum wage was a significant factor in the increase in inequality for lower half of the income distribution.

Who Would Be Affected by a Minimum Wage Increase to $10.10?

According to calculations from the Economic Policy Institute, approximately 28 million workers would see a raise if the minimum wage were raised to $10.10 by July 2016. The affected workers would include not only those making under $10.10 an hour, all of whom would see their wages directly increased, but also those earning just above $10.10. Due to a spillover effect, these workers would see their wages indirectly increased as employers try to maintain the previous relative status of workers in their firms.

The majority of affected workers, those directly and indirectly affected, would be women. Fifty-five percent of the affected workers would be women. For context, women represent 49.2 percent of total employment.

One invalid criticism of the minimum wage as an antipoverty tool is that the minimum wage would primarily benefit teenagers who are working part-time and are supported by their parents. The data, however, do not bear this story out. Contrary to stereotypes of minimum wage workers, 88 percent of affected workers would be adults. A plurality of affected workers, 36.5 percent, would be between the ages of 20 and 29. In fact, the average age of affected workers would be 35 years old.

And the minimum wage increase would not flow mostly to part-time workers. Fifty-three percent of affected workers would work full time, defined as at least 35 hours a week. And research finds that minimum wage hikes do not result in significant decreases in working hours.

Then there are tipped workers, who earn a subminimum wage. They are similar to those who earn the minimum wage as they also are less educated, younger, and more likely to be female than the rest of the workforce. The Harkin-Miller legislation would raise the tipped minimum wage to 70 percent of the regular minimum wage. This increase would give tipped workers a considerable raise from the current tipped minimum wage of $2.13.

The families of minimum wage earners are also dependent upon the earnings of those workers. On average, the earnings of minimum wage earners are 50 percent of their family's incomes.

Comments on CBO's Minimum Wage Report

Overall, the report by the Congressional Budget Office on the proposed minimum wage increases is well done. And that's not a shock considering that it is written by the Congressional Budget Office. Their work is always high quality and a valuable contribution to the policy debate. Yet my reading of the economics literature on the minimum wage leads me to differ with CBO's conclusions. Overall, their report overstates the cost and understates the benefits of increasing the minimum wage, as demonstrated by my written testimony today.

While CBO describes some of its thinking in its selection of employment elasticities from the economics literature, their methodology is relatively vague. They state they favor studies that use a methodology that finds small to no employment effects of modest increases in the minimum wage. They consider publication bias in academic journals that would result in the publication of fewer studies that find no effect. But their preferred elasticities appear to be about halfway between the elasticities found by their stated favored methodology and more negative estimates.

Costs

In several ways, the CBO report overstates the costs of raising the minimum wage with regards to employment. First of all, the report overstates the willingness of employers to substitute workers for capital. Minimum wage jobs are concentrated in industries and occupations where substitution is unlikely. You can't replace a janitor with a Roomba.

The authors also don't account for possible productivity gains from raising the minimum wage. Increased productivity increases wages, but higher wages can boost productivity. Workers who are better paid may become more productive according to the "efficiency wage theory." About 90 percent of interviewed fast food managers, for example, said a minimum wage increase would spur them to help improve the productivity of workers. Worker productivity could also be boosted by reduced turnover due to a minimum wage increase. As workers stay on the job longer they become more familiar with work tasks and therefore more productive.

Finally and perhaps most importantly, the CBO report also doesn't appear to account for the fact that the most price sensitive consumers are also the workers receiving the largest wage gains from an increase in the minimum wage. The low-wage workers who often have the hardest time dealing with price increases would be the ones receiving wage increases. The net effect of a minimum wage increase would be a gain for these workers.

Benefits

The CBO report finds that raising the minimum wage to $10.10 would reduce poverty by 900,000 people. Obviously a reduction in poverty is a good thing, but the report's estimates are almost certainly on the low end of estimates. To calculate the effect of raising the minimum wage on family incomes, CBO uses a simulation to compare wages and incomes after a minimum wage increase to a world where the standard isn't raised.

This method isn't incorrect. But other methods, specifically using historical data, find a much larger reduction in poverty. Simulation methods require assumptions about specific phenomena—like the spillover effect of raising the minimum wage—to be accurate and that there are no measurement errors in the underlying data. A review of the existing literature by University of Massachusetts— Amherst economist Arindrajit Dube on the relationship between the minimum wage and poverty found that the vast majority of the literature finds a negative relationship. On average, these studies find a ten percent increase in the minimum wage reduces the poverty rate by 1.5 percent. Using this conservative elasticity, raising the minimum wage to $10.10 would help raise 2.4 million non-elderly Americans out of poverty. Under Dube's preferred elasticity, the increase in the minimum wage would decrease poverty by 4.6 million non-elderly Americans in the short-term and 6.8 million in the longer term.

Conclusion

The minimum wage is not a silver bullet in the fight against poverty. But any effort to reduce poverty and increase economic mobility at the bottom rungs of the income ladder into the middle class needs to include an increase in the minimum wage. The weight of economic research shows that raising the minimum wage would reduce poverty and work in tandem with other poverty-reducing programs to promote income mobility from the bottom up. In the largest economy on the planet, we need to work harder to reduce poverty. Increasing the minimum wage needs to be part of that effort.

5

Minimum Wages Increase Unemployment

Andrew Syrios

Andrew Syrios is a partner in the real estate investment firm Stewardship Properties.

Just taking a look at recent numbers shows that raising the minimum wage reduces net job growth and has an overall negative effect on employment. It often hurts those it's intended to help by pricing out low-skilled laborers in favor of workers with higher skill sets and degree-based educations. Despite the rallying cry that more money means more opportunity, even the Congressional Budget Office estimates that raising the minimum wage to $10.10 per hour will bleed the U.S. of at least 500,000 jobs.

Raising the minimum wage has become the cause célèbre for many on the progressive left. Most notably, Seattle has passed a $15 per hour minimum wage. In addition, California lawmakers are trying to pass a state-wide $13 per hour minimum wage and President Obama is supporting the increase of the federal minimum wage from $7.25 to $10.10.

The general public has generally been pretty ignorant regarding economics, so it's understandable that many would fall for hollow populist appeals. However, a series of new studies on the minimum wage purport to show a low or non-existent impact on

"Yes, Minimum Wages Still Increase Unemployment," by Andrew Syrios, Mises Institute, February 9, 2015. Reprinted by Permission.

unemployment. Seventy-five notable economists even signed a petition to President Obama to raise the minimum wage.

This would seem at odds with basic economic theory. After all, demand curves are downward sloping, aren't they? At some point, an increase in the minimum wage has got to cost jobs. If the minimum wage was increased to $100 per hour, obviously that would cost a lot of jobs. No one would disagree with this. So in that case, why wouldn't increasing it to $10.10 per hour cost some jobs, right?

Revisionist Studies

Before the latest wave of revisionist studies, the idea that minimum wage hikes don't cause unemployment received a substantial boost in 1994 from a study of New Jersey-Pennsylvania fast food workers. However, David Neumark and William Wascher re-evaluated the evidence and found that the "New Jersey minimum wage increase led to a 4.6 percent decrease in employment in New Jersey relative to the Pennsylvania group."

More recently, the old consensus was challenged again. Robert Murphy summarizes these economists approach as follows:

> If we include regional-specific trends indexed by time period, the influence of the minimum wage begins to disappear and, in particular, using their preferred control group method (of contiguous county pairs) completely obliterates the textbook finding. The minimum wage may even have a positive impact on employment.

However, as Murphy notes, these adjustments "might mask the policy's true effect." As a recent working paper from Jonathan Meer and Jeremy West finds:

> Using three separate state panels of administrative employment data, we find that the minimum wage reduces net job growth, primarily through its effect on job creation by expanding establishments.[1]

In essence, minimum wage increases make it more likely that firms won't hire new people than that they will fire current employees. For example, movie theaters have stopped employing ushers almost entirely. And many companies are moving toward more automation, at least partly because of minimum wage increases.

Furthermore, there is another major problem as Robert Murphy's points out:

> ... careful analysts will often summarize the new research in a nuanced way, saying "modest" increases in the minimum wage appear to have little impact on employment. But the proposed increase from $7.25 to $10.10 an hour is a 39-percent increase, which can hardly be characterized as "modest." Such an increase, therefore, could well destroy teenagers' jobs, notwithstanding the revisionist studies.

It should also be noted that according to the Bureau of Labor Statistics, only "4.3 percent of all hourly paid workers" work at or below the minimum wage and "... workers under the age of 25 ... made up about half of those paid the federal minimum wage or less."[2] Studies focusing on modest increases in the minimum wage are of course not going to show much of a difference. However, even with only modest increases in the minimum wage, effects can be found. As a review of the literature by David Neumark and William Wascher describes:

> Our review indicates that there is a wide range of existing estimates and, accordingly, a lack of consensus about the overall effects on low-wage employment of an increase in the minimum wage. However, the oft-stated assertion that recent research fails to support the traditional view that the minimum wage reduces the employment of low-wage workers is clearly incorrect. A sizable majority of the studies surveyed in this monograph give a relatively consistent (although not always statistically significant) indication of negative employment effects of minimum wages. In addition, among the papers we view as providing the most credible evidence, almost all point to negative employment effects, both for the United States as well as for many other countries.[3]

Indeed, even the Congressional Budget Office estimates that increasing the minimum wage to $10.10 per hour will cost 500,000 jobs.

Hurting Those It's Meant to Help

The minimum wage is constantly sold as good for workers, or minorities or women. In truth, it hurts the most vulnerable and those its well-intentioned sponsors intend to help.

A study by Jeffrey Clemens and Michael Wither evaluated the effect of minimum wage increases on low-skilled workers during the recession and found that minimum wage increases between December 2006 and December 2012 "… reduced the national employment-population ratio by 0.7 percentage points."[4] That amounts to about 1.4 million jobs. And more noteworthy, that "… binding minimum wage increases significantly reduced the likelihood that low-skilled workers rose to what we characterize as lower middle class earnings."

Yes, it's hard to make ends meet with a minimum wage job and such jobs certainly aren't enviable. That being said, cutting out the bottom rung from people just makes it all the harder to get by. A bad job is better than no job and it is often the first step to something better.

[…]

And while the large majority of those pushing for an increase in the minimum wage have good intentions, this has certainly not always been the case. Much like rent controls, increasing the minimum wage reduces the price of discrimination by creating a surplus of laborers for employers to choose from. Whereas many have noted the odd alliance of "Bootleggers and Baptists" when it came to Prohibition, another odd alliance of "Populists and the Prejudiced" could just as easily be applied to the minimum wage.

When Apartheid was collapsing in South Africa, the economist Walter Williams did a study of South African labor markets and found that many white unions were seeking to increase the minimum wage. He quotes one such union leader as saying "… I support the rate for the job (minimum wages) as the second best way of protecting white artisans." By pricing out less educated black laborers with a minimum wage, white unions were able to insulate themselves from competition.

Indeed, the Davis-Bacon Act, which demands that private employers pay "prevailing wages" for any government contracts, was explicitly passed as a Jim Crow law in order to protect white jobs from cheaper black competitors. And while the minimum wage is supported with much more pleasant rhetoric these days, the effects on black employment, particularly black teenage employment, have been devastating. As Thomas Sowell observes,

> In 1948 … the unemployment rate among black 16-year-olds and 17-year-olds was 9.4 percent, slightly lower than that for white kids the same ages, which was 10.2 percent. Over the decades since then, we have gotten used to unemployment rates among black teenagers being over 30 percent, 40 percent or in some years even 50 percent.

It's hard to imagine that black unemployment was actually less than that of whites. But that is the effect minimum wage laws can have.[5]

Ending poverty and giving people additional income are praiseworthy goals, but there are no free lunches in this world. And trying to force prosperity through a minimum wage simply creates a whole host of negative and unintended consequences especially for those who are the most vulnerable.

Notes

1. Jonathan Meer and Jeremy West, "Effects of the Minimum Wage on Employment Dynamics," December 2013, pg. 1.
2. Bureau of Labor Statistics, *Characteristics of Minimum Wage Workers*, 2013, March 2014, pg. 1.
3. David Neumark and William Wascher, "Minimum Wage And Employment: A Review of Evidence From the New Minimum Wage Research," November 2006, pg. 2.
4. Jeffrey Clemens and Michael Wither, "The Minimum Wage and the Great Recession: Evidence on the Employment and Income Trajectories of Low-Skilled Workers," November 24, 2014, pg. 36.
5. In 1948 there was a minimum wage, but because of a high inflation during that decade, it was so low as to be irrelevant.

6

This Is Not About Job Loss

David Howell

David Howell is a professor of economics and public policy and directs the doctoral program in Public and Urban Policy at The New School. He is a faculty research fellow at the Schwartz Center for Economic Policy Analysis, and a research scholar at the Political Economy Research Institute.

The debate over raising the minimum wage and its impact on jobs has been at a stalemate for many years. While there is strong support on both sides of the argument, one perspective indicates that it is unreasonable to impose a no-job loss standard on setting a wage floor. Furthermore, according to experts, the focus on job losses ignores the benefits of higher wages for those that retain their jobs along with the benefits of improving the standard of living for low-wage earners. To connect job loss to wage increases is unfair in both the short term and the long run.

Overview

The leading criticism of the "Fight for $15" campaign to raise the federal minimum wage to $15 an hour is the presumed loss of jobs. Employers, the argument goes, would eliminate some workers or reduce their hours in the short-term, and in the longer run, further automate their operations in order to ensure that they will need fewer low-wage workers in the future. For many leading minimum wage advocates, even a gradually phased-in $12 wage

"The misplaced debate about job loss and a $15 minimum wage," by David Howell, The Washington Center for Equitable Growth, July 6, 2016. Reprinted by Permission.

floor would take us into "uncharted waters" that would be "a risk not worth taking."

On the other side is the long historical concern with making work "pay," even if that means some job loss. In this view, the most important consideration is the overall employment impact on low-wage workers, after accounting for the additional job creation that will come with higher consumer spending from higher wages, which will almost certainly at least offset any direct initial job losses. And even more importantly, what really matters in this view are the likely huge overall net benefits of a large increase for minimum-wage workers and their families.

If we are serious about job opportunities for low-wage workers then there are many effective ways to compensate those who lose their jobs, ranging from expansionary economic policy to increased public infrastructure spending, more generous unemployment benefits and above all, public-sector job creation. A related issue is whether it makes moral, economic and fiscal sense to maintain a low federal minimum wage and then ask taxpayers to subsidize the employers of low-wage workers by propping up the incomes of poor working families only via means-tested programs such as the Earned Income Tax Credit and supplemental nutrition assistance.

The debate has been, effectively, a stalemate, with the federal minimum wage set at extremely low levels ($7.25 since 2008) by both historical and international standards.

Part of the explanation for our persistent failure to establish a minimally decent wage floor at the federal level has been the way the discourse has been framed—even by many of the strongest advocates for substantially higher minimum wage.

In recent years, the best evidence shows that moderate increases from very low wage floors have no discernible effects on employment, which has helped make the case for substantial increases in the minimum wage. But the very strength of this new evidence—research designs that effectively identify employment effects at the level of individual establishments—has contributed to the adoption of a narrow standard for setting the "right" legal wage floor—defined as the wage that previous research demonstrates will pose little or no risk of future job loss, anywhere. For all sides, the central question has become: Whose estimate of the wage threshold at which there is no job losses whatsoever is the most credible?

This policy brief offers a critique of this "no-job-loss" framing in the current debate. I will argue that relying only on statistical estimates of job loss to set the legal floor is inappropriate because these estimates are inherently controversial and unresolveable, because this approach leaves the question to arcane debates among statisticians, and because it fails to account for the net benefits of raising the minimum wage for the majority of workers. The "no-job-loss" framing also misses entirely the moral and ethical reasons for mandating a living wage for low-wage U.S. workers. It sets an impossible standard for making public policy—a standard that rules out any direct short-run job losses anywhere would effectively block most labor, social, and environmental policies and regulations. The remainder of this issue brief unpacks what's wrong with this "no-job-loss" standard.

The Limits of a Purely Statistical Analysis of the Minimum Wage

Identifying the highest minimum wage that poses little or no risk of job losses from econometric evidence of earlier minimum wage increases in other jurisdictions—the main approach—is both extremely challenging and inherently controversial. The current debate consists of a battle over which research designs for which cities, states, or foreign countries most credibly predict what would happen if the federal minimum wage were to be increased over some time frame to, say, $10.10, $12 or $15 an hour. Given the many parties with big stakes in the outcome, relying on a statistically derived wage floor that risks zero job losses all but guarantees endless debates over empirical research.

Some economists, for example, point to existing evidence that the effects on employment when the minimum wage is increased within the $6-to-$10 range are minimal. Yet other researchers continue to argue, with credible statistical support, that sizable increases within this $6-to-$10 range do cause at least some job loss in some establishments in some regions, even if limited to high-turnover teenagers.

But there certainly is no evidence that can be relied upon to identify the no-job-loss threshold for a legal wage floor that would apply to the entire United States—the wage below which it is known that there is little or no risk of job loss anywhere, and above which there is known to be a risk of job loss that is high enough to be not worth taking. The only truly reliable way to do this would be to regularly increase the federal minimum wage while carefully monitoring the employment effects, much as the United Kingdom's Low Pay Commission has done for the minimum wage that was instituted there in 1999.

There are different stakeholders in this debate. On the one side, there are the academic economists who care deeply about empirical confirmation of price-quantity tradeoffs and restaurant owners who care equally as much about their profit margins. On the other side, there are workers and their advocates who desire the establishment of a minimum living wage. Given the many parties with a big stake in the outcome, relying on evidence-based criteria about job loss for setting the wage floor all but guarantees unresolvable controversy.

The Methodological Double Bind in Setting the Minimum Wage

Then there is the methodological problem—a classic case of "Catch 22." Because the identification of the wage at which there is expected to be zero job loss must be evidence-based, there is no way to establish the higher nationwide wage floors necessary for empirical tests. There are other places that have enacted higher minimum wages—think Santa Monica, Seattle, New York state, France, Australia or the United Kingdom—but they would face the same problem if they relied exclusively on zero job loss as the criterion for the proper wage floor. In practice, high minimum wage locations have relied on other criteria when making the political choice to set the legal wage, namely a wage that more closely approximates a minimum living wage than what the unregulated market generates.

In practical terms, local and state government's past reliance on statistical tests for other jurisdictions not only means that we must assume that they are directly applicable (why would evidence from Seattle, New York state or the United Kingdom be a reliable guide to the effects at the level of the entire U.S. labor market?), but also requires that places imposing a no-job-loss standard must always lag far behind the leaders, and effectively condemns them to setting the wage floor well below the actual wage that will start generating job loss. In short, the no-job-loss criterion cannot stand on its own as a coherent and meaningful standard for setting the legal wage floor, and by relying on old statistical results from other places, ensures a wage that is too low on its own terms.

Ignoring the Net Benefits of Raising the Minimum Wage

When the criterion for raising the minimum wage is concerned only with the cost side of an increase, the costs of some predicted job losses are all that matters. If the wage floor is set above the no-job-loss level, what kind of jobs will be lost? Who will be the job losers? What alternatives were available to them? These are the kinds of questions that must be asked to determine the costs of minimum wage related job losses. But there are obviously benefits to raising the legal wage floor. Shouldn't they be counted and compared to the costs?

Those benefits are evident directly for the workers receiving wage increases as a result of a rise in the minimum wage, either because they are earning between the old minimum wage and the new one (say, between $7.25 and $15) or because they earn a bit above the new minimum wage—because employers increase wages to maintain wage differentials among workers by skill or seniority. The benefits also are evident for taxpayers–with a much higher minimum wage there would be less need to rely on means-tested redistribution to increase the after-tax and benefit incomes of working families.

Forgetting the Ethical and Efficiency Arguments for Raising the Minimum Wage

Relying on the no-job-losses criterion for setting an appropriate federal wage floor entirely ignores the main traditional justification for the minimum wage: The moral, social, economic, and political benefits of a much higher standard of living from work for tens of millions of workers. On both human rights and economic efficiency grounds, workers should be able to sustain at least themselves and ideally their families. And on the same grounds, it is preferable to do so from their own work rather than from either tax-based public spending or private charity.

It is hard to put this argument for a living wage better than Adam Smith did several centuries ago:

> A man must always live by his work, and his wages must at least be sufficient to maintain him. They must even upon most occasions be somewhat more; otherwise it would be impossible for him to bring up a family.... No society can surely be flourishing and happy, of which the far greater part of the members are poor and miserable.

A Public Policy Straightjacket

Determining a suitable federal minimum wage based solely on a zero job loss rule is a public policy straightjacket that would effectively rule out any significant raise of the wage floor above that which already exists. Yet from a historical perspective, strict adherence to such policymaking criteria would have also made it impossible to ban child labor (job losses!), as well as many critical environmental and occupational health and safety regulations. It would also foreclose any consideration of policies like paid family leave, which exists in every other affluent country.

Conclusion

Breaking out of this public policy straightjacket requires policymakers to rethink their criteria for raising the minimum wage. It also means that economists must shake off their fear of challenging the prevailing orthodoxy—a no-immediate-harm-to-anyone way of thinking—and see the longer-term benefits to millions of workers. It is estimated that the move to a $15 minimum wage by both California and New York state will directly raise the pay for over one-third of all workers.

If we really care about maximizing employment opportunities then we should not hold a decent minimum wage hostage to the no-job-loss standard. Rather, we should put a much higher priority on full-employment fiscal and monetary macroeconomic policy, minor variations of which would have massively greater employment effects than even the highest statutory wage floors that have been proposed.

But it is also well within our capabilities to counter any job loss that can be linked to the adoption of what the prominent University of Chicago economist J. B. Clark in 1913 called "emergency relief" such as extended unemployment benefits, education and training subsidies, and public jobs programs. A minimum living wage combined with other policies common throughout the affluent world, such as meaningful child-cash allowances, would put the United States back among other rich nations that promote work incentives while all but eliminating both in-work poverty and child poverty. It would put the country into waters that most other affluent nations have charted and are already navigating.

7

Minimum Wage Laws Have Negative Effects

Mark Wilson

Mark Wilson is vice president and chief economist for the HR Policy Association and is the principal of Applied Economic Strategies, LLC. He served as deputy assistant secretary for the Employment Standards Administration at the U.S. Department of Labor.

Economists agree that businesses will make changes to adapt to increases in the minimum wage, but many argue that the higher labor costs will be passed on to someone either through increased prices or reductions in labor. One of the greatest impacts is on teen labor and the working poor. Most studies indicate an adverse effect on employment, and very few studies indicate that raising minimum wages creates positive effects on employment.

The federal government through the Department of Labor has imposed a minimum wage since 1938. Nearly all the state governments also impose minimum wages. These laws prevent employers from paying wages below a mandated level. While the aim is to help workers, decades of economic research show that minimum wages usually end up harming workers and the broader economy. Minimum wages particularly stifle job opportunities for low-skill workers, youth, and minorities, which are the groups that policymakers are often trying to help with these policies.

"The Negative Effects of Minimum Wage Laws," by Mark Wilson, The Cato Institute, September 1, 2012. Reprinted by Permission.

There is no "free lunch" when the government mandates a minimum wage. If the government requires that certain workers be paid higher wages, then businesses make adjustments to pay for the added costs, such as reducing hiring, cutting employee work hours, reducing benefits, and charging higher prices. Some policymakers may believe that companies simply absorb the costs of minimum wage increases through reduced profits, but that's rarely the case. Instead, businesses rationally respond to such mandates by cutting employment and making other decisions to maintain their net earnings. These behavioral responses usually offset the positive labor market results that policymakers are hoping for.

This study reviews the economic models used to understand minimum wage laws and examines the empirical evidence. It describes why most of the academic evidence points to negative effects from minimum wages, and discusses why some studies may produce seemingly positive results.

Some federal and state policymakers are currently considering increases in minimum wages, but such policy changes would be particularly damaging in today's sluggish economy. Instead, federal and state governments should focus on policies that generate faster economic growth, which would generate rising wages and more opportunities for all workers.

Background

The federal minimum wage originated in the Fair Labor Standards Act (FLSA) signed by President Franklin Roosevelt on June 25, 1938. The law established a minimum wage of 25 cents per hour for all employees who produced products shipped in interstate commerce. That wage is equivalent to $4.04 in today's purchasing power.

Originally, the FLSA covered only about 38 percent of the labor force, mostly in the manufacturing, mining, and transportation industries[1]. Over the years, Congress has significantly expanded the coverage and increased the minimum wage rate. The air transport industry was added in 1947, followed by retail trade in 1961. The construction industry, public schools, farms, laundries, and nursing homes were added in 1966, and coverage was extended to state and local government employees in 1974. Currently, the FLSA covers about 85 percent of the labor force[2].

Since 1938 the federal minimum wage has been raised 22 times. From 1949 to 1968 the real value of the minimum wage (in 2011 dollars) rose rapidly from $3.78 to $10.34. At $7.25 per hour, the minimum wage today in real dollars is 85 percent greater than the original benchmark, and just below its average for the past 60 years of $7.59. Since the 1970s, the federal minimum wage has fluctuated around roughly 40 percent of the average private sector hourly wage.

The FLSA requires employers to comply with state minimum wage laws that may set a state minimum wage rate higher than the federal rate[3]. Currently, 45 states and the District of Columbia have their own minimum wages, of which 18 are higher than the current federal minimum of $7.25 per hour[4]. Only five states do not have their own minimum wage laws and rely on the FLSA. Moreover, even state minimum wages that are below the federal minimum often have an effect because they can apply to employers or workers who are exempt from the federal statute.

Who Is Paid the Minimum Wage?

Supporters of minimum wages might believe that these laws mainly help to boost the incomes of full-time adult workers in low-income families, some of whom are supporting children. However, the data generally do not support that view. Most workers earning the minimum wage are young workers, part-time workers, or workers from non-poor families.

According to the Bureau of Labor Statistics, 1.8 million paid-hourly employees were paid the federal minimum wage of $7.25 in 2010[5]. These 1.8 million employees can be broken down into two broad groups:

- Roughly half (49.0 percent) are teenagers or young adults aged 24 or under. A large majority (62.2 percent) of this group live in families with incomes two or more times the official poverty level[6]. Looking just at the families of teenaged minimum wage workers, the average income is almost $70,600, and only 16.8 percent are below the poverty line[7]. Note that the federal minimum wage applies to workers of all ages[8].

- The other half (51.0 percent) are aged 25 and up[9]. More of these workers live in poor families (29.2 percent) or near the poverty level (46.2 percent had family incomes less than 1.5 times the poverty level)[10]. However, even within this half of all minimum wage employees, 24.8 percent voluntarily work part-time, and just 34.3 percent are full-time full-year employees[11].

Only 20.8 percent of all minimum wage workers are family heads or spouses working full time, 30.8 percent were children, and 32.2 percent are young Americans enrolled in school[12]. The popular belief that minimum wage workers are poor adults (25 years old or older), working full time and trying to raise a family is largely untrue. Just 4.7 percent match that description[13]. Indeed, many minimum wage workers live in families with incomes well above the poverty level.

[…]

The Effect of Minimum Wages on Employment

Despite the use of different models to understand the effects of minimum wages, all economists agree that businesses will make changes to adapt to the higher labor costs after a minimum wage increase. Empirical research seeks to determine what changes to variables such as employment and prices firms will make, and how large those changes will be. The higher costs will be passed on to someone in the long run; the only question is who. The important thing for policymakers to remember is that a decision to increase the minimum wage is not cost-free; someone has to pay for it.

The main finding of economic theory and empirical research over the past 70 years is that minimum wage increases tend to reduce employment. The higher the minimum wage relative to competitive-market wage levels, the greater the employment loss that occurs. While minimum wages ostensibly aim to improve the economic well-being of the working poor, the disemployment effects of a minimum wage have been found to fall disproportionately on the least skilled and on the most disadvantaged individuals, including the disabled, youth, lower-skilled workers, immigrants, and ethnic minorities[15].

In his best-selling economics textbook, Harvard University's Greg Mankiw concludes:

> The minimum wage has its greatest impact on the market for teenage labor. The equilibrium wages of teenagers are low because teenagers are among the least skilled and least experienced members of the labor force. In addition, teenagers are often willing to accept a lower wage in exchange for on-the-job training. . . . As a result, the minimum wage is more often binding for teenagers than for other members of the labor force[16].

Research by Marvin Kosters and Finis Welch shows that the minimum wage hurts low-wage workers particularly during cyclical downturns[17]. And based on his studies, Nobel Laureate economist Milton Friedman observed: "The real tragedy of minimum wage laws is that they are supported by well-meaning groups who want to reduce poverty. But the people who are hurt most by higher minimums are the most poverty stricken."[18]

In a generally competitive labor market, employers bid for the most productive workers and the resulting wage distribution reflects the productivity of those workers. If the government imposes a minimum wage on the labor market, those workers whose productivity falls below the minimum wage will find few, if any, employment opportunities. The basic theory of competitive labor markets predicts that a minimum wage imposed above the market wage rate will reduce employment.[19]

Evidence of employment loss has been found since the earliest implementation of the minimum wage. The U.S. Department of Labor's own assessment of the first 25-cent minimum wage in 1938 found that it resulted in job losses for 30,000 to 50,000 workers, or 10 to 13 percent of the 300,000 covered workers who previously earned below the new wage floor.[20] It is important to note that the limited industries and occupations covered by the 1938 FLSA accounted for only about 20 percent of the 30 million private sector, nonfarm, nonsupervisory, production workers employed in 1938. And of the roughly 6 million workers potentially covered by the law, only about 5 percent earned an hourly rate below the new minimum.[21]

Following passage of the federal minimum wage in 1938, economists began to accumulate statistical evidence on the effects. Much of the research has indicated that increases in the minimum wage have adverse effects on the employment opportunities of low-skilled workers.[22] And across the country, the greatest adverse impact will generally occur in the poorer and lower-wage regions. In those regions, more workers and businesses are affected by the mandated wage, and businesses have to take more dramatic steps to adjust to the higher costs.

As an example, with the original 1938 imposition of the minimum wage, the lower-income U.S. territory of Puerto Rico was severely affected. An estimated 120,000 workers in Puerto Rico lost their jobs within the first year of implementation of the new 25-cent minimum wage, and the island's unemployment rate soared to nearly 50 percent.[23]

Similar damaging effects were observed on American Samoa from minimum wage increases imposed between 2007 and 2009. Indeed, the effects were so pronounced on the island's economy that President Obama signed into law a bill postponing the minimum wage increases scheduled for 2010 and 2011.[24] Concern over the scheduled 2012 increase of $0.50, compelled Governor Togiola Tulafono to testify before Congress: "We are watching our economy burn down. We know what to do to stop it. We need to bring the aggressive wage costs decreed by the Federal Government under control... Our job market is being torched. Our businesses are being depressed. Our hope for growth has been driven away."[25] In 1977 ongoing debate about the minimum wage prompted Congress to create a Minimum Wage Study Commission to "help it resolve the many controversial issues that have surrounded the federal minimum wage and overtime requirement since their origin in the Fair Labor Standards Act of 1938."[26] The commission published its report in May 1981, calling it "the most exhaustive inquiry ever undertaken into the issues surrounding the Act since its inception."[27] The landmark report included a wide variety of studies by a virtual "who's who" of labor economists working in the United States at the time.[28]

A review of the economic literature amassed by the Commission by Charles Brown, Curtis Gilroy, and Andrew Kohen found that the "time-series studies typically find that a 10 percent increase in the minimum wage reduces teenage employment by one to three percent."[29] This range subsequently came to be thought of as the consensus view of economists on the employment effects of the minimum wage.

It is important to note that different academic studies on the minimum wage may examine different regions, industries, or types of workers. In each case, different effects may predominate. A federal minimum wage increase will impose a different impact on the fastfood restaurant industry than the defense contractor industry, and a different effect on lowercost Alabama than higher-cost Manhattan. This is why scholarly reviews of many academic studies are important.

In 2006 David Neumark and William Wascher published a comprehensive review of more than 100 minimum wage studies published since the 1990s.[30] They found a wider range of estimates of the effects of the minimum wage on employment than the 1982 review by Brown, Gilroy, and Kohen. The 2006 review found that "although the wide range of estimates is striking, the oft-stated assertion that the new minimum wage research fails to support the traditional view that the minimum wage reduces the employment of low-wage workers is clearly incorrect. Indeed . . . the preponderance of the evidence points to disemployment effects."[31]

Nearly two-thirds of the studies reviewed by Neumark and Wascher found a relatively consistent indication of negative employment effects of minimum wages, while only eight gave a relatively consistent indication of positive employment effects. Moreover, 85 percent of the most credible studies point to negative employment effects, and the studies that focused on the least-skilled groups most likely to be adversely affected by minimum wages, the evidence for disemployment effects were especially strong.

In contrast, there are very few, if any, studies that provide convincing evidence of positive employment effects of minimum wages. These few studies often use a monopsony model to explain these positive effects. But as noted, most economists think such positive effects are special cases and not generally applicable because few low-wage employers are big enough to face an upward-sloping labor supply curve as the monopsony model assumes.[32]

Other Effects of Minimum Wages

Aside from changes in employment, empirical studies have documented other methods by which businesses and markets adjust to minimum wage increases. The congressional Joint Economic Committee published a major review of 50 years of academic research on the minimum wage in 1995.[33] The study found a wide range of direct and indirect effects of increased minimum wages that may occur. These include:

- Increasing the likelihood and duration of unemployment for low-wage workers, particularly during economic downturns;
- Encouraging employers to cut worker training;
- Increasing job turnover;
- Discouraging part-time work and reducing school attendance;
- Driving workers into uncovered jobs, thus reducing wages in those sectors;
- Encouraging employers to cut back on fringe benefits;
- Encouraging employers to install labor-saving devices;
- Increasing inflationary pressure;

- Increasing teenage crime rates as a result of higher unemployment; and
- Encouraging employers to hire illegal aliens.[34]

Another channel of adjustment to minimum wage changes is labor-labor substitution within businesses.[35] Research finds that some employers will replace their lowest-skilled workers with somewhat higher-skilled workers in response to increases in the minimum wage. As a result, minimum wage increases may harm the least skilled workers more than is suggested by the net disemployment effects estimated in many studies because more-skilled workers are replacing some less-skilled workers. Nobel Laureate economist Gary Becker has noted that this effect helps generate political support from labor unions for higher minimum wages: A rise in the minimum wage increases the demand for workers with greater skills because it reduces competition from low-skilled workers. This is an important reason why unions have always been strong supporters of high minimum wages because these reduce the competition faced by union members from the largely non-union workers who receive low wages.[36]

A 2011 study by Barry Hirsch and coauthors found yet further methods of business adjustment.[37] Some firms partially offset increases in the minimum wage by awarding smaller than normal pay increases to their workers who earn more than the minimum wage.

Some firms try to increase worker productivity by requiring better attendance, insisting that job duties are completed faster, imposing additional tasks on workers, minimizing hours worked with better scheduling, and terminating poor performers more quickly.

A final method for businesses to respond to minimum wage increases is to try to push forward the additional costs to consumers. If a minimum wage increase is imposed economywide, it may be partly passed on in prices. However, in a global economy, this is less likely for internationally traded goods because domestic producers facing higher labor costs will be undercut by imports.

So price effects may be more prevalent in goods and services less subject to competition from imports.

In 2004 a comprehensive review of more than 20 minimum wage studies looking at price effects found that a 10 percent increase in the U.S. minimum wage raises food prices by up to 4 percent and overall prices by up to 0.4 percent.[38] A 2007 study from the Federal Reserve Bank of Chicago found that restaurant prices unambiguously increase in response to minimum wage increases.[39] And a 2011 study of quick-service restaurants found that two-thirds of the minimum wage cost increases were offset by higher menu prices, and that higher prices rather than cuts in employment and hours was the most important channel of adjustment for this type of firm.[40]

These results help to reconcile the few minimum wage studies that do not find negative employment effects with the large majority of studies that do. Economic theory suggests that firms can respond to minimum wage increases by reducing employment, raising prices, or both. In the studies that find small or no employment effects, it may be that the businesses studied were able to pass on the added costs solely in higher prices. Indeed, the Federal Reserve study concluded that the results are consistent with the small disemployment effects found in some studies. Note finally that empirical studies finding that minimum wage increases affect prices in some cases is consistent with the competitive model of labor markets, but not with the monopsony model.[41]

Minimum Wages and Poverty

Proposals to increase the minimum wage can be politically popular because they are viewed as being a way of helping the poor. However, evidence from a large number of academic studies suggests that minimum wage increases don't reduce poverty levels. Some of the reasons include:

- Many poor Americans (63.5%) do not work, and thus aren't earning wages.[42]

- Even among the working poor, the relationship between earning a low hourly wage rate and living in poverty is weak and has become weaker over time. That is because most workers who gain from a minimum wage increase live in nonpoor families and most of the working poor already have wages above the required minimums.[43]
- While an increase in the minimum wage will lift some families out of poverty, other low-skilled workers may lose their jobs, which reduces their income and drops their families into poverty.[44]
- If a minimum wage is partly or fully passed through to consumers in the form of higher prices, it will hurt the poor because they disproportionately suffer from price inflation.[45]

Relatively few poor households would benefit from a minimum wage increase even if there were no negative employment or other affects. In the recent federal minimum wage increase from $5.15 to $7.25, only 15.8 percent of the workers who were expected to gain from it lived in poor households.[46] In the current proposal to raise it to $9.50, only 11.3 percent of the workers who would gain live in poor households.[47] And of those who would gain, 63 percent are second or third earners living in households with incomes twice the poverty line.

Since 1995, eight studies have examined the income and poverty effects of minimum wage increases, and all but one have found that past minimum wage hikes had no effect on poverty.[48] One recent academic study found that both state and federal minimum wage increases between 2003 and 2007 had no effect on state poverty rates.[49] These studies generally find that some low-skilled workers living in poor families who remain employed do see their incomes rise. However, other low-skilled workers lose their jobs or have their work hours substantially reduced, which causes income losses and increased poverty. On net, some studies find that the families of low-skilled workers and less-educated single mothers are no better off and may be made worse off by minimum wage hikes.[50] The upshot is that there is no free lunch to this sort of top-down mandated attempt at reducing poverty.

Conclusions

In the American economy, low wages are usually paid to entry-level workers, but those workers usually do not earn these wages for extended periods of time. Indeed, research indicates that nearly two-thirds of minimum wage workers move above that wage within one year.[51] For full-time minimum wage workers, research has found that the median first-year raise is about 14 percent.[52]

While they are often low-paid, entry-level jobs are vitally important for young and low-skill workers because they allow people to establish a track record, to learn skills, and to advance over time to a better-paying job. Thus, in trying to fix a perceived problem with minimum wage laws, policymakers cause collateral damage by reducing the number of entry-level jobs. As Milton Friedman noted, "The minimum wage law is most properly described as a law saying employers must discriminate against people who have low skills."[53]

Seventy years of empirical research generally finds that the higher the minimum wage increase is relative to the competitive wage level, the greater the loss in employment opportunities. A decision to increase the minimum wage is not cost-free; someone has to pay for it, and the research shows that low-skill youth pay for it by losing their jobs, while consumers may also pay for it with higher prices. Moreover, evidence from a large number of academic studies shows that, even if there were no negative employment or other affects, minimum wage increases don't reduce poverty levels. Only 11.3 percent of the workers who would gain from a recent proposal to increase the minimum wage to $9.50 an hour even live in poor households.[54]

Some current proposals on Capitol Hill and at the state level to raise minimum wages could not come at a worse time. The current unemployment rate for teenagers is 24.9 percent, and this group's employment rate is near its record low of 25.4 percent. For minority youth the situation is even worse. The unemployment rate for minority teenagers is 38.2 percent, and the employment rate is just 15.5 percent.

In these tough economic conditions, employers are simply not going to hire workers whose labor produces less than the cost of hiring them. Employers will not pay $8.25 an hour to hire a worker whose hourly efforts bring in $7.25. A higher minimum wage will price even more low-skilled individuals out of a job. Although a small share of workers will get a raise, others will lose opportunities for employment. Minimum wages generally don't distribute income to workers from employers, but to a small group of lucky workers from the unlucky workers who lose jobs.

Rather than pursuing policies such as minimum wage increases that create winners and losers, policymakers should focus on policies that generate faster economic growth to benefit all workers. While minimum wages may be a well-meaning attempt to help workers, economic research clearly shows that somebody must pay the price for any increase, and it is usually the least skilled and least fortunate among us.

Notes

1 Finis Welch, "Minimum Wages: Issues and Evidence," American Enterprise Institute, 1978.

2 The self-employed are the largest group of workers not covered by the Fair Labor Standards Act, followed by federal employees and certain transportation employees.

3 Fair Labor Standards Act, 29 USC 218(a).

4 U.S. Department of Labor, Wage and Hour Division, "Minimum Wage Laws in the States—January 1, 2012," www.dol.gov/whd/minwage/america.htm.

5 Bureau of Labor Statistics, "Characteristics of Minimum Wage Workers: 2010," February 25, 2011,www.bls.gov/cps/minwage2010.pdf.

6 Author's analysis of the Bureau of Labor Statistic's Current Population Survey data for March 2010.

7 Author's analysis of the Bureau of Labor Statistic's Current Population Survey data for March 2010.

8 A minor exception is the 90-day "training" wage of $4.25 per hour allowed for youth under age 20. After the 90-day period, youth must be paid the full minimum wage.

9 Author's analysis of the Bureau of Labor Statistic's Current Population Survey data for March 2010.

10 Author's analysis of the Bureau of Labor Statistic's Current Population Survey data for March 2010.

11 Author's analysis of the Bureau of Labor Statistic's Current Population Survey data for March 2010.

12 Author's analysis of the Bureau of Labor Statistic's Current Population Survey data for March 2010.

13 Author's analysis of the Bureau of Labor Statistic's Current Population Survey data for March 2010.

15 "Standard economic theory predicts that minimum wage increases do not reduce profits because low wage firms are usually too small and too competitive to absorb the extra costs. It is then not surprising that empirical evidence is scanty on profit effects." Sara Lemos, "The Effect of the Minimum Wage on Prices," Institute for the Study of Labor (Germany), Discussion Paper no. 1072, March 2004.

16 Mankiw quotes from his textbook at Greg Mankiw, "The Minimum Wage Debate," April 23, 2006,http://gregmankiw.blogspot.com.

17 Marvin Kosters and Finis Welch, "The Effects of Minimum Wages on the Distribution of Changes in Aggregate Employment," *American Economic Review* 62, no. 3 (June 1972): 323–32. See also Finis Welch, "Minimum Wage Legislation in the United States," *Economic Inquiry* 12, no. 3 (September 1974): 285–318.

18 Milton Friedman, quoted in Keith B. Leffler, "Minimum Wages, Welfare, and Wealth Transfers to the Poor,"*Journal of Law and Economics* 21, no. 2 (October 1978): 345–58.

19 Randall K. Filer, Daniel S. Hamermesh, and Albert E. Rees, *The Economics of Work and Pay*, (New York: HarperCollins, 1996).

20 Thomas Rustici, "A Public Choice View of the Minimum Wage," *Cato Journal* 5, no. 1 (Spring-Summer 1985): 103–31. Rustici points out that the DOL's estimates of job losses were likely too low. He cites reports that in Texas alone the imposition of the minimum wage dislocated 40,000 workers from pecan-shelling plants. The introduction of mechanical pecanshelling equipment, which replaced manual shelling, closely followed the implementation of the minimum wage, despite the fact that the automated process produced a lower quality product (more broken nuts and shell pieces).

21 The total labor force in 1938 was about 54 million, including agricultural, self-employed, government, professional, administrative, and managerial workers, as well as unemployed persons.

22 Robert S. Goldfarb, "The Policy Content of Quantitative Minimum Wage Research," Proceedings of the Industrial Relations Research Association, 27th Annual Meeting, San Francisco, December 28–29, 1974.

23 Thomas Rustici, "A Public Choice View of the Minimum Wage," *Cato Journal* 5, no. 1 (Spring-Summer 1985): 103–31.

24 Public Law 111-244, September 30, 2010.

25 Governor Togiola Tulafono, testimony before the Subcommittee on Fisheries, Wildlife, Oceans and Insular Affairs, House Committee on Natural Resources, "The Impact of Minimum Wage Increases on American Samoa," September 23, 2011.

26 Minimum Wage Study Commission, Report of the Minimum Wage Study Commission, (Washington: Government Printing Office, 1981), vol. 1, p. xiii.

27 Minimum Wage Study Commission, Report of the Minimum Wage Study Commission, (Washington: Government Printing Office, 1981), vol. 1, letter of transmittal.

28 David Neumark and William L. Wascher, *Minimum Wages* (Cambridge, MA: MIT Press, 2008).

29 Charles Brown, Curtis Gilroy, and Andrew Kohen, "The Effect of the Minimum Wage on Employment and Unemployment," *Journal of Economic Literature* 20, no. 2 (June 1982): 487–528. This research survey was a substantial revision of the previous work the authors conducted for the Minimum Wage Study Commission.

30 David Neumark and William Wascher, "Minimum Wages and Employment: A Review of Evidence from the New Minimum Wage Research," National Bureau of Economic Research, Working Paper no. 12663, November 2006.

31 David Neumark and William Wascher, "Minimum Wages and Employment: A Review of Evidence from the New Minimum Wage Research," National Bureau of Economic Research, Working Paper no. 12663, November 2006.

32 Madeline Zavodny, "Why Minimum Wage Hikes May Not Reduce Employment," Federal Reserve Bank of Atlanta,Economic Review, Second Quarter 1998.

33 Joint Economic Committee, "50 Years of Research on the Minimum Wage," February 15, 1995,http://web.archive.org/web/20110629183749/http://www.house.gov/jec/cost-....

34 Joint Economic Committee, "50 Years of Research on the Minimum Wage," February 15, 1995,http://web.archive.org/web/20110629183749/http://www.house.gov/jec/cost-....

35 Joint Economic Committee, "50 Years of Research on the Minimum Wage," February 15, 1995,http://web.archive.org/web/20110629183749/http://www.house.gov/jec/cost-....

36 Gary Becker, "On Raising the Federal Minimum Wage," November 26, 2006, www.becker-posner-blog.com.

37 Barry T. Hirsch, Bruce E. Kaufman, and Tetyana Zelenska, "Minimum Wage Channels of Adjustment," Institute for the Study of Labor (Germany), Discussion Paper no. 6132, November 2011.

38 Sara Lemos, "The Effect of the Minimum Wage on Prices," Institute for the Study of Labor (Germany), Discussion Paper no. 1072, March 2004.

39 Daniel Aaronson, Eric French, and James MacDonald, "The Minimum Wage, Restaurant Prices, and Labor Market Structure," Federal Reserve Bank of Chicago, WP 2004-21, rev. August 3, 2007.

40 Barry T. Hirsch, Bruce E. Kaufman, and Tetyana Zelenska, "Minimum Wage Channels of Adjustment," Institute for the Study of Labor (Germany), Discussion Paper no. 6132, November 2011.

41 Daniel Aaronson and Eric French, "Output Prices and the Minimum Wage," Employment Policies Institute, June 2006.

42 Author's analysis of the Bureau of Labor Statistic's Current Population Survey data for March 2010.

43 Richard V. Burkhauser and Joseph J. Sabia. "The Effectiveness of Minimum Wage Increases in Reducing Poverty: Past, Present, and Future," *Contemporary Economic Policy* 25, no. 2 (April 2007).

44 Richard V. Burkhauser and Joseph J. Sabia, "Minimum Wages and Poverty: Will a $9.50 Federal Minimum Wage Really Help the Working Poor?" *Southern Economic Journal* 77, no. 3 (January 2010).

45 Sara Lemos, "The Effect of the Minimum Wage on Prices," Institute for the Study of Labor (Germany), Discussion Paper no. 1072, March 2004.

46 Sara Lemos, "The Effect of the Minimum Wage on Prices," Institute for the Study of Labor (Germany), Discussion Paper no. 1072, March 2004.

47 Sara Lemos, "The Effect of the Minimum Wage on Prices," Institute for the Study of Labor (Germany), Discussion Paper no. 1072, March 2004.

48 Sara Lemos, "The Effect of the Minimum Wage on Prices," Institute for the Study of Labor (Germany), Discussion Paper no. 1072, March 2004.

49 Sara Lemos, "The Effect of the Minimum Wage on Prices," Institute for the Study of Labor (Germany), Discussion Paper no. 1072, March 2004.

50 Sara Lemos, "The Effect of the Minimum Wage on Prices," Institute for the Study of Labor (Germany), Discussion Paper no. 1072, March 2004. See also Richard Vedder and Lowell Gallaway, "Does the Minimum Wage Reduce Poverty?" Employment

Policies Institute, June 2001; Jill Jenkins, "Minimum Wages: The Poor Are Not Winners," Employment Policy Foundation, January 12, 2000; and Ronald B. Mincy, "Raising the Minimum Wage: Effects on Family Poverty," *Monthly Labor Review* 113, no. 7 (July 1990).
51 William Even and David Macpherson, "Rising Above the Minimum Wage," Employment Policies Institute, January 2000.
52 William Even and David Macpherson, "Rising Above the Minimum Wage," Employment Policies Institute, January 2000.
53 Interview with Milton Friedman, "Living Within Our Means," Richard Heffner's Open Mind, December 7, 1975,www.thirteen.org/openmind/public-affairs/living-within-ourmeans/ 494/.
54 Richard V. Burkhauser and Joseph J. Sabia, "Minimum Wages and Poverty: Will a $9.50 Federal Minimum Wage Really Help the Working Poor?" *Southern Economic Journal* 77, no. 3 (January 2010).

8

Minimum Wage Means Maximum Potential

David Cooper and Doug Hall

David Cooper is a senior economic analyst at the Economic Policy Research Institute where he conducts national and state-level research. He is also deputy director of EPI's Economic Analysis and Research Network (EARN).

Doug Hall is director of the Economic Policy Institute's Economic Analysis and Research Network (EARN).

T he idea persists that raising the minimum wage would provide multiple positive effects on the overall economy. Researchers claim it would boost the earnings of low-wage families and would provide economic stimulus through increased consumer spending. In turn, these studies show, that increased consumer spending and the resulting economic stimulus would create much-needed jobs. Thus, it's imperative to boost wages to foster a nation-wide boom and take the U.S. to where it needs to be in the world market.

By highlighting the need to increase the federal minimum wage in his State of the Union address, President Obama breathed new life into a critically important issue. Wages for U.S. workers, particularly low-wage workers, have eroded not just in recent years, but over several decades (Mishel 2013; McNichol et al. 2012). This erosion has contributed to the growth of income inequality, leaving the economy less vibrant than if incomes were distributed more evenly. Raising the minimum wage and incorporating a system for automatic adjustment over time is key to reversing this erosion of low-wage workers' earnings, and would help combat growth of income inequality.

Following the president's expression of support for a $9.00 minimum wage, Sen. Tom Harkin (D-Iowa) and Rep. George Miller (D-Calif.) indicated their support for increasing the minimum wage to $10.10 (this proposal follows their 2012 effort to pass legislation supporting a $9.80 minimum wage). Their proposal—now formalized as S.460, the Fair Minimum Wage Act of 2013—would increase the minimum wage via three incremental increases of $0.95, and then index it to inflation, so that as prices rise, so would the minimum wage. Also, the tipped minimum wage (the minimum wage paid to workers who earn a portion of their wages in tips) would be increased in $0.85 increments from its current value of $2.13 per hour, where it has languished since 1991, until it reaches 70 percent of the regular minimum wage.

Raising the minimum wage would help reverse the ongoing erosion of wages that has contributed significantly to growing income inequality. At the same time, it would provide a modest stimulus to the entire economy, as increased wages would lead to increased consumer spending, which would contribute to GDP growth and modest employment gains.

This paper begins by examining the minimum wage in context, noting where the minimum wage would be today had it grown at the same rate as other important benchmarks over the last few decades. It then provides a demographic overview of the workers who would benefit from the proposed minimum-wage increase, examining characteristics such as their gender, age, race and ethnicity, educational attainment, work hours, family income, and family composition. Next, it details the estimated GDP and job creation impacts that would result from increasing the federal minimum wage to $10.10.

Key findings include:

- Increasing the federal minimum wage to $10.10 by July 1, 2015, would raise the wages of about 30 million workers, who would receive over $51 billion in additional wages over the phase-in period.[1]
- Across the phase-in period of the minimum-wage increase, GDP would increase by roughly $32.6 billion, resulting in the creation of approximately 140,000 net new jobs (and 284,000 job years) over that period.
- Those who would see wage increases do not fit some of the stereotypes of minimum-wage workers.
  - Women would be disproportionately affected, comprising 56 percent of those who would benefit.
  - Over 88 percent of workers who would benefit are at least 20 years old.
  - Although workers of all races and ethnicities would benefit from the increase, non-Hispanic white workers comprise the largest share (about 54 percent) of those who would be affected.
  - About 44 percent of affected workers have at least some college education.
  - Around 55 percent of affected workers work full time, 70 percent are in families with incomes of less than $60,000, more than a quarter are parents, and over a third are married.
  - The average affected worker earns about half of his or her family's total income.

The Minimum Wage in Context

President Obama noted in his most recent State of the Union address that a parent who is a minimum-wage worker and works full time, year round, does not earn enough to be above the federal poverty line. This was not always the case. **Figure A** shows the annual earnings of a minimum-wage worker compared with the federal poverty line for a family of two or three. Until the 1980s, earning the minimum wage was enough to lift a single parent out of poverty. Indeed, a minimum-wage income in 1968 was higher than the poverty line for a family of two adults and one child. But as the figure shows, today's minimum wage is not enough for single parents to reach even the most basic threshold of adequate living standards.

Figure A. Poverty levels for minimum-wage-earning families of two or three, 1964-2012

Note: Poverty thresholds are 2012 levels for families of two (one adult, one child) and three (two adults, one child). Note that the poverty threshold for a family of one adult, two children is slightly higher ($18,498). Annual earnings are calculated assuming workers work full time (40 hours per week) and 52 weeks per year (i.e., with no vacation). Minimum wage is deflated using CPI-U-RS.

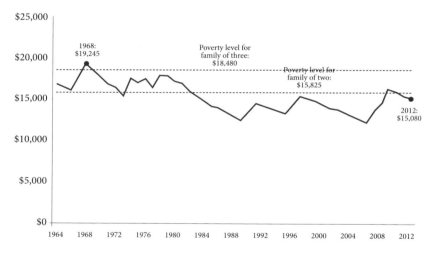

SOURCE: Author's analysis of U.S. Census Bureau and U.S. Department of Labor Wage and Hour Division

Moreover, the gap between the minimum wage and the average wage of production and nonsupervisory workers used to be much smaller. **Figure B** shows the minimum wage as a percentage of the average wage. Through the 1960s, minimum-wage workers earned about 50 percent of what the average American production worker earned. Over time, as the value of the minimum wage has eroded, the wage gap between minimum-wage workers and the average American wage earner has grown to the point where, today, a minimum-wage worker earns only 37 percent of the average wage.

Figure B. Minimum wage as percentage of average wage

Note: The average wage is the average hourly wage of production and non-supervisory workers.

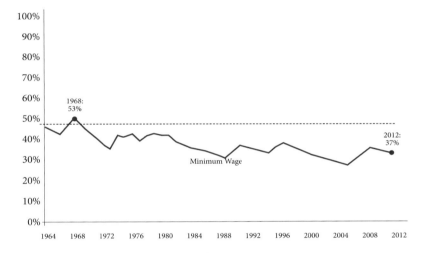

SOURCE: Author's analysis of data from Current Population Survey and U.S. Department of Labor Wage and Hour Division

Over the last 45 years, minimum-wage workers have not seen the benefits of a growing economy. As productivity has increased and the economy has expanded, our capacity to generate income and raise overall living standards has grown dramatically. Yet the minimum wage has been left to stagnate, effectively preventing the country's lowest-paid workers from sharing in this increased prosperity. **Figure C** depicts the actual value of the minimum wage over time, compared with what it might have been under three alternative scenarios.

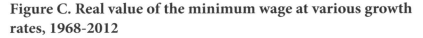

Figure C. Real value of the minimum wage at various growth rates, 1968-2012

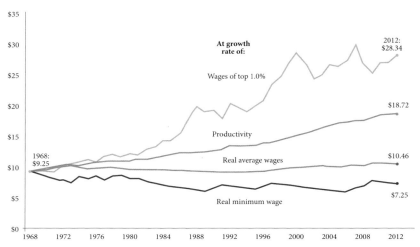

SOURCE: Authors' analysis of data from Social Security Administration wage statistics; Total Economy Productivity Data from the Bureau of Labor Statistics Labor Productivity and Costs program; Bureau of Labor Statistics Current Employment Statistics; and U.S. Department of Labor Wage and Hour Division

As the figure shows, if the minimum wage had kept pace with average wages—i.e., if minimum-wage workers' paychecks had expanded at the same rate as average workers'—it would be about $10.50 today. If the minimum wage had kept pace with productivity[2]—i.e., the economy's overall capacity to generate income—it would be almost $18.75 today. Finally, if the minimum wage had increased at the same rate as wages of the top 1.0 percent, it would be over $28 per hour.[3]

Demographic Characteristics of Affected Workers

Increasing the minimum wage to $10.10 would benefit millions of workers whose characteristics—in terms of their gender, age, race and ethnicity, educational attainment, work hours, family income, and family composition—contradict some prevailing beliefs about minimum-wage workers. In the first year, with an increase from $7.25 to $8.20, 14 million directly and indirectly affected workers would see higher wages. This number would rise to about 21 million workers with the second incremental increase to $9.15 in 2014, and to more than 30 million workers with the third incremental increase to $10.10 in 2015, as shown in **Figure D**.[4] As detailed later in this section, the vast majority of these workers are not teenage part-time workers; rather, most are at least 20 years old, over half work full time, and many are struggling to support their families.

Figure D. Workers (in millions) affected by increasing the federal minimum wage

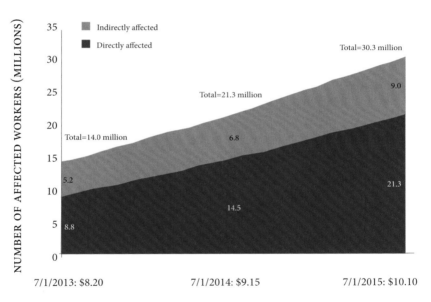

SOURCE: Authors' analysis of Harkin/Miller proposal using Current Population Survey Outgoing Rotation Group

Gender

Raising the minimum wage is a women's issue. While increasing the minimum wage would have a sizable impact on both men and women, it would disproportionately affect women. Women comprise 49.4 percent of U.S. workers, yet 56.0 percent of workers who would be affected by a potential minimum-wage increase (**see Figure E**). The share of those affected who are women varies somewhat by state, from a low of 51 percent in California (and 47.8 percent in the District of Columbia) to a high of 64.9 percent in Mississippi.[5]

Figure E. Workers affected by increasing federal minimum wage, by gender

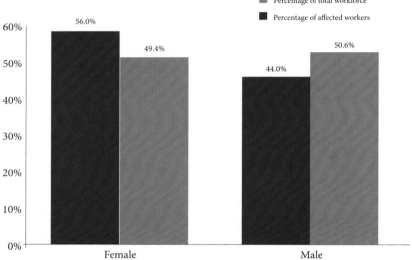

SOURCE: Authors' analysis of Harkin/Miller proposal using Current Population Survey Outgoing Rotation Group

Age

Minimum-wage workers are older and, as discussed later, have greater family responsibilities than commonly portrayed. The facts do not support the perception of minimum-wage workers as primarily teenagers working for spending money (though even if true, it would not justify paying teens subpoverty wages).

Instead, as seen in **Figure F**, 88.3 percent of workers who would be affected by increasing the federal minimum wage to $10.10 are at least 20 years old. This share varies from a low of 79.4 percent in New Hampshire to 94.4 percent in Louisiana (and 94.6 percent in the District of Columbia). Thus, in every state, more than three-fourths of workers who would be affected are at least 20 years old.

Figure F. Workers affected by federal minimum wage, by age

SOURCE: Authors' analysis of Harkin/Miller proposal using Current Population Survey Outgoing Rotation Group

Race/Ethnicity

Increasing the minimum wage would substantially benefit both minority and nonminority workers. **Figure G** reveals that nationally, 54.1 percent of workers who would be affected are non-Hispanic white workers. Nearly a quarter (24.6 percent) are Hispanic, 14.1 percent are black, and 7.1 percent are Asian or of another race or ethnicity.

Figure G. Workers affected by increasing federal minimum wage, by race

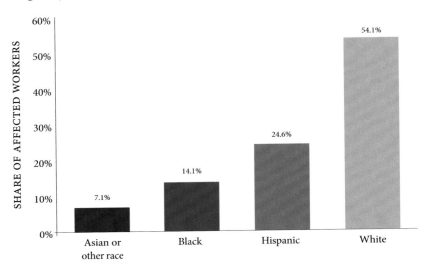

SOURCE: Authors' analysis of Harkin/Miller proposal using Current Population Survey Outgoing Rotation Group

As one would expect given the country's diverse social and cultural makeup, the racial and ethnic composition of workers affected by increasing the federal minimum wage to $10.10 varies considerably by state:

- The Asian or other race/ethnicity composition ranges from 1.7 percent in West Virginia to 75.9 percent in Hawaii.
- The black composition ranges from less than 1 percent in Idaho, Montana, and New Hampshire to 46.5 percent in Mississippi (and 57.1 percent in the District of Columbia).
- The Hispanic composition ranges from 0.9 percent in West Virginia to 58.6 percent in California.
- The white composition ranges from 10.7 percent in Hawaii to 93.5 percent in Maine.

Educational Attainment

Data on educational attainment of those who would be affected by a minimum-wage increase further dispel the misperception of minimum-wage workers as high school students. In fact, nationally just 21.3 percent of those who would be affected have less than a high school degree, while fully 43.8 percent have some college education, an associate degree, or a bachelor's degree or higher (see **Figure H**). This share ranges from 37.8 percent in Texas (and 34.4 percent in the District of Columbia) to 53.6 percent in Massachusetts.

Figure H. Workers affected by increasing federal minimum wage, by education level

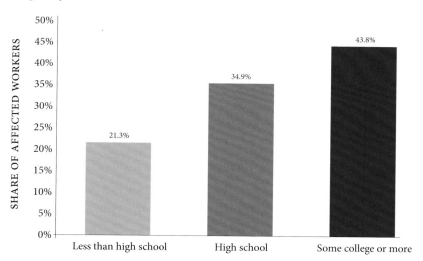

SOURCE: Authors' analysis of Harkin/Miller proposal using Current Population Survey Outgoing Rotation Group

Work Hours

Among those who would be affected by increasing the minimum wage to $10.10, only 14.2 percent are part-time workers (defined as those who work less than 20 hours per week). More than half (54.5 percent) work full time (35 or more hours per week), while 31.3 percent work mid-time, between 20 and 34 hours per week.

Southern states generally have a much smaller share of affected workers who work part time. The states with the lowest shares include Mississippi (7.8 percent), Arkansas (8.7 percent), and Louisiana (8.8 percent). (The District of Columbia's share stands at 8.6 percent.) States with the highest shares of affected workers who work part time include states primarily concentrated in the North, led by New Hampshire (26.9 percent), Vermont (25.0 percent), and Minnesota (23.9 percent).

Family Income

The family income of those who would be affected by a minimum-wage increase is generally low to moderate...70.0 percent of affected families have a total family income of less than $60,000, and nearly a quarter (23.2 percent) have total family income of less than $20,000. Among all U.S. families, the median family income in 2011 was $61,455 (according to data from the American Community Survey).

The share of families affected by increasing the federal minimum wage to $10.10 with family income under $60,000 varies considerably by state, from nearly half (47.6 percent) in New Hampshire to more than four-fifths in Arkansas (83.6 percent), Mississippi (82.9 percent), and Montana (82.6 percent).

Those who would be affected by increasing the minimum wage to $10.10 are vital contributors to their families' earnings. Nationally, the average affected worker earns half (49.9 percent) of his or her family's total income. This percentage varies from a low of 32.9 percent in New Hampshire to a high of 61.4 percent in Mississippi.

Family Composition

Nationally, over a quarter (27.9 percent) of those who would be affected by increasing the minimum wage to $10.10 are parents, while over a third (35.8 percent) are married (according to an analysis of Current Population Survey Outgoing Rotation Group microdata). Moreover, of the 75 million children in the United States, nearly a quarter (23.3 percent) have a parent who would benefit from the proposed federal minimum-wage increase. This percentage varies from 12.9 percent in Alaska to 31.5 percent in Texas. Eight other states where over a quarter of children have a parent who would benefit from the minimum-wage increase include Idaho (29.4 percent), Arkansas (28.5 percent), Mississippi (28.1 percent), Kansas (26.7 percent), South Carolina (26.5), Tennessee (26.4 percent), Georgia (25.6 percent), and Indiana (25.5 percent). Of the nine states where more than a quarter of children have an affected parent, all but Idaho, Kansas, and Indiana had child poverty rates of 25 percent or more in 2011 (Annie E. Casey Foundation 2012), highlighting the importance of boosting their family incomes by raising the minimum wage.

In short, a minimum-wage increase would boost the wages of a diverse multitude of American workers—and would thus have widespread economic benefits. The following section details the magnitude of these economic effects.

Raising the Minimum Wage as a Tool for Economic Growth

The immediate benefits of a minimum-wage increase are in the boosted earnings of the lowest-paid workers, but its positive effects would far exceed this extra income. Recent research reveals that, despite skeptics' claims, raising the minimum wage does not cause job loss.[6] In fact, throughout the nation, a minimum-wage increase under current labor market conditions would create jobs. Like unemployment insurance benefits or tax breaks for low and middle-income workers, raising the minimum wage puts more money in the pockets of working families when they need it most, thereby augmenting their spending power. Economists generally recognize that low-wage workers are more likely than any other income group to spend any extra earnings immediately on previously unaffordable basic needs or services.

Increasing the federal minimum wage to $10.10 by July 1, 2015, would give an additional $51.5 billion over the phase-in period to directly and indirectly affected workers[7], who would, in turn, spend those extra earnings. Indirectly affected workers—those earning close to, but still above, the proposed new minimum wage—would likely receive a boost in earnings due to the "spillover" effect (Shierholz 2009), giving them more to spend on necessities. This projected rise in consumer spending is critical to any recovery, especially when weak consumer demand is one of the most significant factors holding back new hiring (Izzo 2011).[8] Though the stimulus from a minimum wage increase is smaller than the boost created by, for example, unemployment insurance benefits, it has the crucial advantage of not imposing costs on the public sector.

[…]

Conclusion

The multiple positive effects that would result from a higher minimum wage are clear: It would boost the earnings of working families hardest hit by the Great Recession, spur economic growth, and create about 140,000 net new jobs. In an economic climate in which wage increases for the most vulnerable workers are scarce, raising the minimum wage to $10.10 by July 1, 2015, is an opportunity that America's working families cannot afford to lose.

Endnotes

1. The phase-in period modeled for this report would commence upon enactment of the initial minimum-wage increase (assumed in this study to be July 1, 2013) and run through June 30, 2016, though there is no way to precisely allocate the distribution of the GDP impact and related job creation following each incremental increase in the minimum wage.

2. Here, productivity refers to total economy productivity.

3. Inflation projections were made using the Congressional Budget Office's inflation projections for the Consumer Price Index. Productivity, average wages, and wages of the top 1.0 percent were projected out from their 2012 or 2011 values at the average annual growth rate for each series from 2002 to 2006, the last full regular business cycle.

4. These data, and the data presented throughout this issue brief, include directly affected workers (those who would see their wages rise because the new minimum wage would exceed their current hourly pay) and indirectly affected workers (those who would receive a raise as employer pay scales are adjusted upward to reflect the higher minimum wage).

5. These, and all other national and state-level demographic statistics, were generated through the authors' analysis of Current Population Survey Outgoing Rotation Group microdata from the Bureau of Labor Statistics.

6. See the EPI paper *The Benefits of Raising Illinois' Minimum Wage: An Increase Would Help Working Families and the State Economy* (Hall and Gable 2012) or *Why Does the*

Minimum Wage Have No Discernible Effect on Employment? (Schmitt 2012) for a summary of the definitive studies on minimum-wage increases and the absence of disemployment effects.

7. The increased wages are the annual amount of increased wages for directly and indirectly affected workers, assuming they work 52 weeks per year.

8. In a poll of 53 economists by *Wall Street Journal*, the majority (65 percent) cited a lack of demand as the main reason for a lack of new hiring by employers (Izzo 2011).

References

American Community Survey. 2012. "Table B19119—Median Family Income in the Past 12 Months." Generated using American Fact Finder. http://factfinder2.census.gov/faces/tableservices/jsf/pages/productview.xhtml?pid=ACS_11_1YR_B19119&prodType=table

Annie E. Casey Foundation. 2012. *2012 KIDS COUNT Data Book: State Trends in Child Well-Being*. Baltimore: Annie E. Casey Foundation.

Bivens, L. Josh. 2011. *Method Memo on Estimating the Jobs Impact of Various Policy Changes*. Economic Policy Institute. http://www.epi.org/publication/methodology-estimating-jobsimpact/

Bureau of Labor Statistics (U.S. Department of Labor) Current Employment Statistics program. Various years. Employment, Hours, and Earnings—National [database]. http://www.bls.gov/ces/#data

Bureau of Labor Statistics (U.S. Department of Labor) Labor Productivity and Costs program. Various years. Major Sector Productivity and Costs and Industry Productivity and Costs [databases]. http://www.bls.gov/lpc/#data. (Unpublished data provided by program staff at EPI's request.)

Current Population Survey Outgoing Rotation Group microdata. Various years. Survey conducted by the Bureau of the Census for the Bureau of Labor Statistics [machine-readable microdata file]. Washington, D.C.: U.S. Census Bureau. http://www.bls.census.gov/ftp/cps_ftp.html#cpsbasic

Hall, Doug, and Mary Gable. 2012. *The Benefits of Raising Illinois' Minimum Wage: An Increase Would Help Working Families and the State Economy*. Economic Policy Institute, Issue Brief #321. http://www.epi.org/publication/ib321-illinoisminimum- wage/

Izzo, Phil. 2011. "Dearth of Demand Seen behind Weak Hiring." *Wall Street Journal*, July 18. http://online.wsj.com/ article/ SB10001424 052702303661904576452181063763332.html

Kopczuk, Wojciech, Emmanuel Saez, and Jae Song. 2010. "Earnings Inequality and Mobility in the United States: Evidence from Social Security Data Since 1937." *Quarterly Journal of Economics*, February. http://elsa.berkeley.edu/~saez/ kopczuk-saez-songQJE10mobility.pdf

McNichol, Elizabeth, Hall, Douglas, Cooper, David and Vincent Palacios. 2012. *Pulling Apart: A State-by-State Analysis of Income Trends*. Economic Policy Institute and Center on Budget and Policy Priorities. http://www.epi.org/publication/ pulling-apart-2012/

Mishel, Lawrence. 2013. *Declining Value of the Federal Minimum Wage Is a Major Factor Driving Inequality*. Economic Policy Institute, Issue Brief #351. http://www.epi.org/ publication/ declining-federal-minimum-wage-inequality/

Powell, Michael. 2011. "Corporate Profits Are Booming. Why Aren't the Jobs?" *New York Times*, January 8. http://www.nytimes. com/2011/01/09/weekinreview/ 09powell.html

Schmitt, John. 2013. *Why Does the Minimum Wage Have no Discernible Effect on Employment?* Center for Economic and Policy Research. http://www.cepr.net/documents/publications/ min-wage-2013-02.pdf

Shierholz, Heidi. 2009. *Fix It and Forget It: Index the Minimum Wage to Growth in Average Wages*. Economic Policy Institute, Briefing Paper #251. http://www.epi.org/publication/bp251/

Shierholz, Heidi, 2013. "Job Openings and Hiring Dropped in December, and Have Not Increased Since Early 2012." Economic Policy Institute JOLTS report, February 12. http://www.epi.org/ publication/job-seekers-ratio-february- 2013/

Social Security Administration. Wage Statistics. Various years. Wage Statistics [database]. http://www.ssa.gov/cgi-bin/ netcomp.cgi

U. S. Census Bureau. 2012. "Poverty Thresholds by Size of Family and Number of Children." [Excel file] https://www.census.gov/hhes/ www/poverty/data/threshld/ index.html

U.S. Department of Labor, Wage and Hour Division. 2012. "History of Federal Minimum Wage Rates Under the Fair Labor Standards Act, 1938-2009." http://www.dol.gov/whd/ minwage/chart.htm

U.S. Senate. 113th Congress. 2013. "S.460: Fair Minimum Wage Act of 2013."

Zandi, Mark. 2011. "At Last, the U.S. Begins a Serious Fiscal Debate." Dismal Scientist (Moody's Analytics' subscription-based website), April 14. http://www.economy.com/dismal/article_free.asp?cid= 198972&tid=F0851CC1-F571-48DE-A136-B2F622EF6FA4

9

Raising Minimum Wage Doesn't Change Anything

David Neumark

David Neumark is professor of economics and director of the Center for Economics and Public Policy at the University of California, Irvine.

While some studies have indicated that, when looking at narrow geographic comparisons of the impact of minimum wage increases, the effect on employment is close to zero, follow-up studies have suggested that such geographic limitations generate misleading evidence. The overall body of research indicates that a higher minimum wage results in some job loss for low-skilled workers, which results in a less than favorable outlook for minimum wage reform.

The minimum wage has gained momentum among policymakers as a way to alleviate rising wage and income inequality. Much of the debate over this policy centers on whether raising the minimum wage causes job loss, as well as the potential magnitude of those losses. Recent research shows conflicting evidence on both sides of the issue. In general, the evidence suggests that it is appropriate to weigh the cost of potential job losses from a

Reprinted from the Federal Reserve Bank of San Francisco's "The Effects of Minimum Wages on Employment," Federal Reserve Bank of San Francisco, Economic Letter 2015-37, December 21, 2015. The opinions expressed in this viewpoint do not necessarily reflect the views of the management of the Federal Reserve Bank of San Francisco or of the Board of Governors of the Federal Reserve System. http://www.frbsf.org/economic-research/publications/economic-letter/2015/december/effects-of-minimum-wage-on-employment/.

higher minimum wage against the benefits of wage increases for other workers.

It is easy to be confused about what effects minimum wages have on jobs for low-skilled workers. Researchers offer conflicting evidence on whether or not raising the minimum wage means fewer jobs for these workers. Some recent studies even suggest *overall* employment could be harmed. This *Letter* sheds light on the range of estimates and the different approaches in the research that might explain some of the conflicting results. It also presents some midrange estimates of the aggregate employment effects from recent minimum wage increases based on the research literature.

The Controversy Begins with the Theory

The standard model of competitive labor markets predicts that a higher minimum wage will lead to job loss among low-skilled workers. The simplest scenario considers a competitive labor market for a single type of labor. A "binding" minimum wage that is set higher than the competitive equilibrium wage reduces employment for two reasons. First, employers will substitute away from the low-skilled labor that is now more expensive towards other inputs, such as equipment or other capital. Second, the higher wage and new input mix implies higher prices, in turn reducing product and labor demand.

Of course, the labor market is more complicated. Most important, workers have varying skill levels, and a higher minimum wage will lead employers to hire fewer low-skilled workers and more high-skilled workers. This "labor-labor" substitution may not show up as job losses unless researchers focus on the least-skilled workers whose wages are directly pushed up by the minimum wage. Moreover, fewer jobs for the least-skilled are most important from a policy perspective, since they are the ones the minimum wage is intended to help.

In some alternative labor market models, worker mobility is limited and individual employers therefore have some discretion in setting wages. In such "monopsony" models, the effect of increasing the minimum wage becomes ambiguous. However, such models may be less applicable to labor markets for unskilled workers most affected by the minimum wage; these markets typically have many similar employers in close proximity to each other (think of a shopping mall) and high worker turnover. Nonetheless, the ultimate test is not theoretical conjecture, but evidence.

Recent Research on Employment Effects of Minimum Wages

The earliest studies of the employment effects of minimum wages used only national variation in the U.S. minimum wage. They found elasticities between −0.1 and −0.3 for teens ages 16–19, and between −0.1 and −0.2 for young adults ages 16–24. An elasticity of −0.1 for teens, for example, means that a 10% increase in the wage floor reduces teen employment by 1%. Newer research used data from an increasing number of states raising their minimum wages above the federal minimum. The across-state variation allowed comparisons of changes in youth employment between states that did and did not raise their minimum wage. This made it easier to distinguish the effects of minimum wages from those of business cycle and other influences on aggregate low-skill employment. An extensive survey by Neumark and Wascher (2007) concluded that nearly two-thirds of the more than 100 newer minimum wage studies, and 85% of the most convincing ones, found consistent evidence of job loss effects on low-skilled workers.

Research since 2007, however, has reported conflicting findings. Some studies use "meta-analysis," averaging across a set of studies to draw conclusions. For example, Doucouliagos and Stanley (2009) report an average elasticity across studies of −0.19, consistent with earlier conclusions, but argue that the true effect is closer to zero; they suggest that the biases of authors and journal editors make it more likely that studies with negative estimates will be published. However, without strong assumptions it is impossible to rule out an alternative interpretation—that peer review and publication lead to more evidence of negative estimates because the true effect is negative. In addition, meta-analyses do not assign more weight to the most compelling evidence. Indeed, they often downweight less precise estimates, even though the lower precision may be attributable to more compelling research strategies that ask more of the data. In short, meta-analysis is no substitute for critical evaluation of alternative studies.

A second strand of recent research that conflicts with earlier conclusions argues that geography matters. In other words, the only valid conclusions come from studies that compare changes among close or contiguous states or subareas of states (for example, Dube, Lester, and Reich 2010). A number of studies using narrow geographic comparisons find employment effects that are closer to zero and not statistically significant for both teenagers and restaurant workers. The studies argue that their results differ because comparisons between distant states confound actual minimum wage effects with other associated negative shocks to low-skill labor markets.

Some follow-up studies, however, suggest that limiting comparisons to geographically proximate areas generates misleading evidence of no job loss effects from minimum wages. Pointing to evidence that minimum wages tend to be raised when labor markets are tight, this research suggests that, among nearby states that are similar in other respects, minimum wage increases are more likely to be associated with positive shocks, obscuring the actual negative effects of minimum wages. Using better methods to pick appropriate comparison states, this research finds negative elasticities in the range of -0.1 to -0.2 for teenagers, and smaller elasticities for restaurant workers (see Neumark, Salas, and Wascher 2014a,b, and Allegretto et al. 2015 for a rebuttal). Other analyses that try to choose valid geographic comparisons estimate employment responses from as low as zero to as high as -0.50 (Baskaya and Rubinstein 2012; Liu, Hyclak, and Regmi 2015; Powell 2015; Totty 2015).

Some new strategies in recent studies have also found generally stronger evidence of job loss for low-skilled workers. For example, Clemens and Wither (2014) compare job changes within states between workers who received federal minimum wage increases because of lower state minimums and others whose wages were low but not low enough to be directly affected. Meer and West (2015) found longer-term dynamic effects of minimum wages on job growth; they suggest these longer-term effects arise because new firms are more able to choose labor-saving technology after a minimum wage increase than existing firms whose capital was "baked in."

How do we summarize this evidence? Many studies over the years find that higher minimum wages reduce employment of teens and low-skilled workers more generally. Recent exceptions that find no employment effects typically use a particular version of estimation methods with close geographic controls that may obscure job losses. Recent research using a wider variety of methods to address the problem of comparison states tends to confirm earlier findings of job loss. Coupled with critiques of the methods that generate little evidence of job loss, the overall body of recent evidence suggests that the most credible conclusion is a higher minimum wage results in some job loss for the least-skilled workers—with possibly larger adverse effects than earlier research suggested.

Recent Minimum Wage Increases and Implications

Despite the evidence of job loss, policymakers and the voting public have raised minimum wages frequently and sometimes substantially in recent years. Since the last federal increase in 2009, 23 states have raised their minimum wage. In these states, minimum wages in 2014 averaged 11.5% higher than the federal minimum (Figure 1). If these higher minimum wages have in fact lowered employment opportunities, this could have implications for changes in aggregate employment over this period.

Figure 1. Difference in state and federal minimum wages, June 2014

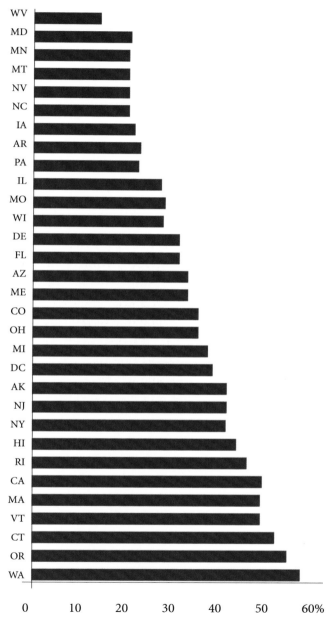

Note that more states (31) had minimums above the federal level just before the Great Recession than do now (Figure 2). The average relative to the federal minimum was nearly three times as high at 32.3%. However, this is in part because the federal minimum wage has increased 41% since the beginning of 2007. To compare the average change across states between 2007 and 2014, I

Figure 2. Difference in state and federal minimum wages, June 2007

account for the smaller number of states with higher minimums in 2014 and their lower levels, and weight the states by their working-age population. I find that minimum wages were roughly 20.6% higher in 2014 than in 2007, compared with a 16.5% increase in average hourly earnings over the same period. Thus, between the federal increases in 2007–09 and recent state increases, the minimum wage has grown only slightly faster than average wages in the economy—around 4.1% over the entire seven-year period.

From the research findings cited earlier, one can roughly translate these minimum wage increases into the overall job count. Among the studies that find job loss effects, estimated employment elasticities of −0.1 to −0.2 are at the lower range but are more defensible than the estimates of no employment effects. Some of the larger estimates are from studies that are likely to receive more scrutiny in the future.

Using a −0.1 elasticity and applying it only to teenagers implies that higher minimum wages have reduced employment opportunities by about 18,600 jobs. An elasticity of −0.2 doubles this number to around 37,300. If we instead use the larger 16–24 age group and apply the smaller elasticity to reflect that a smaller share of this group is affected, the crude estimate of missing jobs rises to about 75,600. Moreover, if some very low-skilled older adults also are affected (as suggested by Clemens and Wither 2014), the number could easily be twice as high, although there is much less evidence on older workers.

Thus, allowing for the possibility of larger job loss effects, based on other studies, and possible job losses among older low-skilled adults, a reasonable estimate based on the evidence is that current minimum wages have directly reduced the number of jobs nationally by about 100,000 to 200,000, relative to the period just before the Great Recession. This is a small drop in aggregate employment that should be weighed against increased earnings for still-employed workers because of higher minimum wages. Moreover, weighing employment losses against wage gains raises the broader question of how the minimum wage affects income inequality and poverty.

References

Allegretto, Sylvia, Arindrajit Dube, Michael Reich, and Ben Zipperer. 2015. "Credible Research Designs for Minimum Wage Studies: A Response to Neumark, Salas, and Wascher." Unpublished manuscript.

Baskaya, Yusuf Soner, and Yona Rubinstein. 2012. "Using Federal Minimum Wage Effects to Identify the Impact of Minimum Wages on Employment and Earnings across U.S. States." Unpublished paper, Central Bank of Turkey.

Clemens, Jeffrey, and Michael Wither. 2014. "The Minimum Wage and the Great Recession: Evidence of Effects on the Employment and Income Trajectories of Low-Skilled Workers." NBER Working Paper 20724.

Doucouliagos, Hristos, and T.D. Stanley. 2009. "Publication Selection Bias in Minimum-Wage Research? A Meta-Regression Analysis." *British Journal of Industrial Relations* 47(2), pp. 406–428.

Dube, Arindrajit, T. William Lester, and Michael Reich. 2010. "Minimum Wage Effects Across State Borders: Estimates Using Contiguous Counties." *Review of Economics and Statistics* 92(4), pp. 945–964.

Liu, Shanshan, Thomas J. Hyclak, and Krishna Regmi. 2015. "Impact of the Minimum Wage on Youth Labor Markets." *Labour*, early publication online.

Meer, Jonathan, and Jeremy West. 2015. "Effects of the Minimum Wage on Employment Dynamics." *Journal of Human Resources*, early publication online.

Neumark, David, J.M. Ian Salas, and William Wascher. 2014a. "More on Recent Evidence on the Effects of Minimum Wages in the United States." *IZA Journal of Labor Policy* 3(1).

Neumark, David, J.M. Ian Salas, and William Wascher. 2014b. "Revisiting the Minimum Wage-Employment Debate: Throwing Out the Baby with the Bathwater?" *Industrial and Labor Relations Review* 67(Supplement), pp. 608–648.

Neumark, David, and William Wascher. 2007. "Minimum Wages and Employment." *Foundations and Trends in Microeconomics* 3(1–2), pp. 1–182.

Powell, David. 2015. "Synthetic Control Estimation beyond Case Studies: Does the Minimum Wage Decrease Teen Employment?" Unpublished manuscript.

Totty, Evan. 2015. "The Effect of Minimum Wages on Employment: A Factor Model Approach." Unpublished manuscript.

10

A Living Wage Is a Local Economy's Lifeblood

Jeff Chapman and Jeff Thompson

Jeff Chapman is Director of Economic Development, State Fiscal Health and Economic Growth at The Pew Charitable Trusts.

Jeffrey P. Thompson is a principal economist on the Board of Governors of the Federal Reserve System.

Research reveals that, at the municipal level, living wage laws have small to moderate effects on municipal budgets. Moreover, studies indicate that the actual costs of such ordinances tend to be lower than the estimated costs, and living wage laws at the local level have raised productivity and decreased turnover. Though controversy about national impact is constantly brewing, the small-scale benefits cannot be ignored or dismissed out of hand.

The modern living wage movement was born in Baltimore in 1994, when the city passed an ordinance requiring firms to pay employees a rate above the minimum wage while working on city contracts. Since then, over 120 communities have followed suit, some setting wage floors more than twice the federal minimum wage, and some requiring various benefits.

The astounding growth of the living wage movement has been a response to the predicament of Americans who work but are unable to make ends meet, as well as to the public policies contributing to the problem.

"The economic impact of local living wages," by Jeff Chapman and Jeff Thompson, Economic Policy Institute, February 15, 2006. Reprinted by Permission.

Public policies have exacerbated the problem from the federal level to the local level. Since the early 1980s, the federal government has generally neglected the minimum wage; by 2005, a minimum wage paycheck bought less than it had in 49 of the last 50 years. Local governments have contributed to the problem, following the trend of cutting costs by contracting out services to firms who frequently pay lower wages and offer fewer benefits than public employment. Too often, economic development efforts have channeled public funds in the form of tax breaks or tax incentives to businesses without regard to the quality of the jobs those businesses provide.

As a result of these policies, the two most common themes echoed by living wage proponents are (1) that wages should be high enough to allow workers to meet basic needs (i.e., "living wages"), and (2) that municipal policy should encourage or require living wages for its employees and contractors, rather than exacerbate the problems faced by low-wage workers.

Despite having common goals, living wage laws vary considerably in practice. Most cover employees working under municipal contracts. Some also cover municipal employees, employees of businesses receiving public economic development dollars, or employees of businesses located in districts that have benefited from significant public investment. Wage levels vary from one dollar above the federal minimum wage to over twice the minimum. Some exempt nonprofit organizations, while others primarily affect human service providers.

One characteristic most share is considerable scrutiny—by pushing for higher wages and challenging the way municipal governments operate, living wage policies have generated significant interest from many different parties. One of the chief concerns among all observers has been the economic effects for municipalities, workers, and firms.

Using the growing body of research that has empirically determined the actual effects of living wage policies, this study shows that:

Living wage laws have small to moderate effects on municipal budgets.

- A detailed survey of 20 cities found that the actual budgetary effect of living wage laws had been consistently overestimated by city administrators; actual costs tended to be less than one-tenth of 1% of the overall budget.
- Two separate studies of the Baltimore living wage found that city contract costs increased less than the rate of inflation.
- A study of the Los Angeles ordinance found no measurable effect on the city's fiscal health.
- A study of living wage ordinances in three New England cities found that contract costs only rose in one city.
- Multiple studies have shown that the bidding for municipal contracts remained competitive or even improved as a result of living wage ordinances.

Living wage laws benefit working families with few or no negative effects.

- Recent studies using original surveys in both Los Angeles and Boston have shown that the workers affected were mostly adults and mostly working full time.
- Both the Boston and Los Angeles studies also showed that most living wage workers were in households struggling to meet a basic-needs budget.
- In Baltimore and Boston, empirical studies have found no evidence of diminished employment.
- In Los Angeles, surveys of workers and firms show that job losses affected just 1% of workers getting a raise.
- Two studies of San Francisco living wage policies found employment increased among airport workers and home health care workers.
- An exception to the general conclusion of research on living wages is a series of studies by David Neumark and

Scott Adams that estimate relatively large wage gains and employment losses. The method of these studies has been severely criticized, and the findings discredited by many researchers.

Living wages laws have raised productivity and decreased turnover among affected firms.

- Multiple studies of Baltimore, Boston, Los Angeles, and San Francisco have shown that firms enjoy lower turnover among employees as a result of the living wage ordinance.
- A study of home-care workers in San Francisco found that turnover fell by 57% following implementation of a living wage policy.
- A study of the Los Angeles ordinance found that absenteeism declined, and the decrease in turnover offset 16% of the total cost of the living wage ordinance.
- A study of the San Francisco airport found that annual turnover among security screeners fell from 95% to 19%, as their hourly wage rose from $6.45 to $10.00 an hour.

[...]

Effects of Living Wage Ordinances on Workers

Living wage workers

The characteristics of workers who benefit have always been of interest to researchers studying the effects of living wage ordinances. Because of the policy's stated goals, information on the demographics and family income of the workers receiving raises is relevant when judging success.

The Los Angeles Alliance for a New Economy conducted a survey in 2002 of 320 randomly selected workers who benefited from the Los Angeles living wage ordinance. This survey proved to be a rich data source for information on the thousands of workers who received raises, showing that:

- 96% were age 20 and older; 58% were 35 and older
- 86% worked full time
- 71% had only a high school degree or less
- On average, workers had been in the workforce nearly 20 years
- 29% were African American
- 57% were female

The LAANE survey did not provide reliable family income data. Instead, LAANE analyzed a similar group of low-wage workers from the Current Population Survey, finding that 69% fell below a "basic needs" budget (Fairris et al. 2005, 38).[9]

Brenner and Luce surveyed 97 low-wage workers employed in the industries most affected by Boston's living wage policy.[10] The survey of this group of covered workers reveals a generally similar profile as Los Angeles:

- Workers were predominantly adult, full-time workers, who were disproportionately people of color[11]
- The average age of covered workers in Boston was 32, with 95% age 20 or older (Brenner and Luce 2005, 51-52)
- 40% of covered workers were African American, and 79% were female
- The average covered worker worked 43 hour per week (Brenner and Luce 2005, 60)

Workers benefiting from the Boston living wage policy were also disproportionately poor and low-income, especially prior to its implementation. Among those covered workers getting a wage increase under the ordinance, over half (54%) were from households with incomes too low to afford even a basic needs budget. [12]

One difference between the affected workers in Boston and Los Angeles is the level of education. Among workers impacted by Boston's living wage, 37% had only a high school degree or less, compared to 71% in Los Angeles (Fairris et al. 2005, 31). More than half of covered workers in Boston had a two- or four-year degree, and 11% had a master's degree (Brenner and Luce, 51). The reason for this difference is that the Boston ordinance primarily covers nonprofit social service providers (a workforce with relatively low wages and relatively high educational attainment), while the workers impacted by the Los Angeles ordinance primarily work at the airport and in a variety of service contract jobs for the city.

In the study of the San Francisco airport, Reich also reports some basic demographic characteristics of affected workers. Following the implementation of the QSP, more than three-quarters of affected workers were 25 or older, and 86% were non-white[13] (Reich 2005, 134).

Employment effects

A frequently expressed concern about living wage ordinances is that the increased cost might decrease employment opportunities for low-skilled workers by causing employers to hire fewer workers or even lay off employees. The employment impact of living wage ordinances is a primary focus of most recent living wage studies. In attempting to answer the question of whether or not living wage ordinances have a significant impact on employment, different researchers have used a variety of approaches, ranging from qualitative interviews with service contractors and affected workers, to detailed before-and-after analysis of impacted firms, to econometric analyses of readily available labor market data. Most of the available studies have concluded that there have been either no or only small employment losses as a result of adopting living wages.

At the time when the earliest analyses were conducted, there was not enough data to quantitatively assess the impact that living wage laws had on employment. Instead, researchers relied on qualitative surveys to develop an impression of the potential impacts on employment. In their 1996 study, researchers from Preamble interviewed 31 contractors affected by the wage increase. None of the firms, including the janitorial services most heavily impacted by the increase, reported reducing staffing levels as a result of the living wage requirement (Preamble 1996, 10). In 1999, Niedt interviewed 26 workers employed in jobs affected by the Baltimore living wage ordinance. Based on questions about conditions at their workplaces, Niedt concluded there was "no evidence that employment levels or working time had changed because of the living wage" (Niedt 1999, 27). Later studies have used quantitative data and more sophisticated techniques to answer the question about employment impacts, and have reached similar conclusions as these early studies.

In his post-passage study of the Boston living wage, Brenner found little evidence of job losses. There was no significant difference in changes in employment (total employment or full-time equivalent (FTE) employment) between contractors who were forced to raise wages because of the law and those that did not have to raise wages (Brenner 2005, 73). For example, affected firms added 22.1 FTE positions, while unaffected firms added 22.4.[14] Also, the number of contract employees covered by the Boston ordinance increased more at firms that were forced to raise wages to comply than those that did not have to raise wages. Brenner's study documents that while approximately 1,000 workers received wage gains, there was no evidence of reduced employment or hours.[15]

The Los Angeles living wage ordinance directly raised the wages of an estimated 7,700 workers, according to the LAANE study[16] (Fairris et al. 2005, 20). This extensive study, using original surveys of firms and workers, found that job loss occurred for less than 1% of the covered workers, or 1.4% of those receiving mandatory wage increases. On the firm side, less than one in five affected firms reported making any staffing changes due to the living wage.[17]

The analysis by Reich et al. of the living wage policy at the San Francisco Airport concluded that there was no evidence of employment losses due to the policy. Despite a recession-induced decline in airport activity by early 2001, SFO employment in jobs covered by the QSP rose by more than 15% between 1998 and 2001—the period in which the QSP was implemented (Reich 2005,

129). As Reich et al. report, "this increase is surprising given that over the same period, airport activity declined by 9% and overall employment in the San Francisco [metropolitan area] increased by only 1%."[18]

Although her research focuses primarily on employee turnover, Candace Howes' findings from her study of the living wage ordinance for home-care workers in San Francisco also does not support claims of job loss. Over the four years of her study (late 1997-early 2002), the number of home-care workers increased by 54% (Howes 2002, 2).

A series of studies by Neumark and Adams are an exception to the general findings of studies of employment effects. They report significant decreases in employment as a result of cities adopting living wage policies. In at least five separate papers, Neumark and Adams examine the effects of living wage laws by comparing the experience of the lowest-paid workers in cities with living wage laws to those in cities without such laws.[19] In each of their studies, Neumark and Adams report that the workers in living wage cities have experienced positive wage effects, but negative effects on employment relative to workers in non-living wage cities.

While Neumark and Adams' research has received wide attention, it has also been criticized by a number of economists, especially work by Brenner, Wicks-Lim, and Pollin. While it is not possible to fully address all of the criticisms in this review, below is a brief summary.

To begin with, the data source used in the Neumark and Adams studies is the Current Population Survey (CPS), a national survey used by the Bureau of Labor Statistics to measure unemployment, wages, and other labor market outcomes. While an excellent data source for many purposes, it is inappropriate for the task of analyzing the impact of living wage laws. Given that in some communities the living wage law only impacts a few hundred workers, it is unlikely that any affected workers are surveyed by the CPS at all in some communities. Even in Los Angeles, with one of the broadest of living wage ordinances, Brenner, Wicks-

Lim, and Pollin estimate that one year of CPS data would likely include about eight affected workers[20] (Brenner, Wicks-Lim, and Pollin 2002, 13). In addition, the CPS does not contain data on the workers' employer, making it impossible to positively identify those eight workers if they do appear in the survey. Using the CPS to analyze the economic effects of living wage laws makes finding a needle in a haystack look like a relatively simple chore, which is why most researchers have eschewed it for the more costly and time-intensive process of administering new surveys targeted specifically to be able to calculate the impacts of living wages. These surveys reflect the experiences of firms and workers actually impacted by living wage ordinances, while the CPS data at best allow Neumark and Adams to analyze a broad swath of the more general, low-wage workforce.

Neumark and Adams report that their findings are driven by laws that extend the living wage requirement to firms who are recipients of business assistance (such as tax breaks). They report that laws that only cover employees working on municipal contracts (the majority of policies) do not have significant impacts on wages or employment. The finding that laws covering business assistance drive the results casts doubt on the studies because most observers believe the business assistance extensions to be weakly implemented or even redundant. Brenner et al. have argued that a large share of the cities with business assistance provisions had not actually implemented this part of the law during the time studied by Neumark and Adams; while these provisions exists on paper, firms have not actually been required to raise wages because of them.[21] Economic development expert Timothy Bartik considers the effects identified by Neumark and Adams unrealistic since, "large economic development subsidies typically only go to new and expanding manufacturing companies...[which]...are a small share of the labor market and pay high enough wages that few workers would be affected by living wages" (Bartik 2004, 290). Bartik's assessment is supported by Elmore's survey, which found that "many business subsidy programs already emphasized attracting high-wage jobs, so living wage laws effectively formalized and reinforced existing practices" (Elmore 2003, 2).

In order to rule out the possibility that their findings were spurious, Neumark and Adams calculated the wage and employment effects for two groups of workers they call "covered" and "non-covered" workers. Since living wage beneficiaries cannot be identified directly in the CPS, they used a classification scheme that ends up including unreasonably large portions of the workforce—over 85% of the lowest-paid one-fourth of workers in cities with living wage ordinances are classified as "covered" (Neumark 2002, 60). Referring to the Los Angeles example, Fairris estimates that fewer than 10,000 workers benefited from the living wage ordinance, but Neumark's and Adams' classification scheme proceeds as if approximately 450,000 workers received a raise under the ordinance![22]

The size of the poverty reduction effects reported by Neumark and Adams are also simply too large given that living wage ordinances affect relatively few workers (Bartik 2004, 290). Similarly, the disemployment effect reported by Neumark and Adams is unrealistic, equivalent to 91% of the total number of workers most other researchers have estimated to be affected (Fairris and Reich 2005, 10).

Brenner et al. found that Neumark and Adams' key findings are extremely sensitive to the inclusion of workers from Los Angeles earning less that the state minimum wage.[23] Since most firms affected by the Los Angeles ordinance are also covered by the state's minimum wage and can generally be expected to be in compliance with it, it is doubtful that workers not covered by the minimum wage would be "potentially covered" by the living wage law.[24]

Because of these factors, it is unlikely that the differences in wages, employment, and poverty between the two groups of cities (living wage and non-living wage) are due to living wage ordinances. As Richard Freeman notes, "any of a host of uncontrolled factors that change the economy in an area exclusive of a living wage ordinance could explain the empirical patterns [observed by Neumark and Adams]" (Freeman 2005, 24).

All told, Neumark and Adams' results are simply not believable. Their econometric analysis shows that, on average, metropolitan areas with "business assistance" provisions tended to have more negative employment outcomes and more positive wage outcomes than other cities during the time studies. For all of the reasons discussed above, however, there is little reason to believe that these results are capturing the effects of living wage ordinances. The effects measured by Neumark and Adams are too large to be reasonable, the data source they use is inadequate to capture what they are hoping to measure, and there are too many other possible factors that could be driving their findings.

In summary, the best empirical research has shown that the adoption of higher wage floors has not resulted in measurable employment loss. Yet many prospective studies predict the opposite. While some predictions of job losses resulting from living wage ordinances have been based on perfectly defensible, if not empirically supported reasoning, others are simply re-treads from different debates that are not actually relevant to living wage ordinances. One such argument is that firms will relocate to avoid having to pay a living wage. This is a standard (and generally unproven) argument in the debate over minimum wage laws, but it is not relevant to living wage ordinances. Living wage policies, particularly the predominant contractor-only variety, are typically not place-based policies. A service contractor can elect to not submit bids for future contracts should they not wish to abide by the living wage mandate.

As long as they continue to contract, however, they will be covered by the law regardless of whether they relocate or not. For the few living wage ordinances that are place-based (in that they apply to firms leasing public facilities), it is either not feasible to relocate (airlines) or the geographic region of application is so narrow that firm relocation would not necessarily imply job loss for a city even if such relocation made sense (airport concessionaires or firms leasing other types of public facilities). In any event, estimates provided by Pollin suggest that the costs imposed on firms from living wage ordinances are too low to justify relocation as a feasible response even if it were possible to dodge the living wage ordinance requirements by doing so (Pollin 2005). In Los Angeles, 81% of firms that were forced to raise wages did not cut any jobs, in large part because "either the number of workers affected was small or the size of the required raises was minimal" (Fairris et al. 2005, 95).

The absence of predicted job losses is due in part to the small impact of living wage policy on employers, and also that some of the costs faced by employers have been offset by increased spending by municipal governments. Although such cost increases are much lower than frequently predicted, as discussed in the previous section, they have occurred to some degree and have softened the blow to contractors accordingly.

In addition, there are details of specific living wage ordinances (as opposed to the general principle behind wage floors) that might limit job losses. In their study of the Baltimore living wage ordinance, Niedt identifies that the specific nature of the major school bus contracts makes it almost impossible to reduce either worker hours or employment levels. As Niedt explains, "the bus routes have not changed and cannot be drastically sped up, nor can an aide work on more than one bus at a time" (Niedt 1999, 19). Also concerning Baltimore, the Preamble study notes that some of the large janitorial contracts have mandatory staffing levels that the firms cannot alter even if they want to (Preamble 1998, 12). In Los Angeles, the LAANE study shows that contractually determined staffing levels also prevented job losses at parking firms as well as airline service contractors (Fairris et al. 2005, 95).

Other studies have identified that living wage ordinances in some municipalities apply to large numbers of nonprofit/ human services organizations. Although nonprofits are exempted altogether in some living wage ordinances and almost entirely in others, they are covered in some cities. Because of their nonprofit status and strict limits on uses of some funding sources, nonprofits may respond differently to living wage ordinances than for-profit enterprises. As Brenner notes in his study of the Boston ordinance, nonprofits may go to greater lengths to avoid layoffs in the face of labor cost increases from a mandated wage increase (Brenner and Luce 2005).

Implementation and enforcement
The only way for workers to benefit from living wage laws is if they are covered by laws that are implemented and enforced. If few workers are covered and/or policies are not actually implemented or enforced, there is little reason to think that workers will gain.

Regarding implementation and enforcement, there have been problems for living wage ordinances from the very beginning. Even after adopting the first living wage ordinance in Baltimore, it took many months, rallies, public hearings, complaints, and fines before some firms started to obey the law. As Stephanie Luce has documented, major post-passage struggles have been required in several cities before the law was implemented. Based on extensive interviews with city administrators, living wage advocates, and review of newspaper reporting on living wage laws, Luce considers more than half of all living wage ordinances to have been only "narrowly" implemented[25] (Luce 2005, 45). As she explains:

> In some places, implementation seems to simply fall through the cracks: there is no single person in charge and no one who knows much about the ordinance. There are other cities in which the staff is incompetent, ineffective, or personally opposed to the ordinances. There are also cities where the administration is outwardly opposed to the ordinance and works to stall implementation, water down, or repeal the laws. Finally, some city councilors and/or administrators continue to publicly support living wage ordinances but make it easy for employers to receive waivers or exemptions from coverage (Luce 2005, 46).

In their study of the Los Angeles living wage ordinance, Sander and Lokey found that enforcement, compliance, and discipline were all problems. Firms did not submit required paperwork, site visits were not performed, and no action was taken against contractors violating the policy. In their 18-month review of the ordinance, Sander and Lokey considered the discipline process to be "toothless," and one of several implementation problems limiting the effect of the ordinance (Sander and Lokey 1998, 4). Sander and Lokey did indicate, however, that by late 1998 most implementation issues were improving. More recent work by LAANE indicates that, as of 2001-02, virtually all firms surveyed were in compliance with the wage requirements, but there may be problems with compliance with other provisions.

Finally, some living wage ordinances, even if they are implemented and enforced, have such narrow coverage that they raise the wages of few workers. This is a general problem with living wage ordinances around the country. Living wage ordinances end up being narrow in scope because some sectors are excluded from coverage (nonprofits, for example). Small contracts are also usually exempted from coverage, with small being defined as anywhere from under $10,000 to under $100,000. Also, small contractors, only partly related to the size of the contract, are sometimes exempted, based on number of employees or firm revenues.

Some cities also exempt contractors based on the source of their funding. In the first year of the Los Angeles ordinance, 59% of potentially covered contracts were granted exemptions, many because the contract was funded with federal resources, which the city was allocating or "passing through" (Sander and Lokey 1998, 2). Some ordinances apply only to those employees directly working on the contract, while others set a threshold, applying only to workers putting in more than a certain portion of their work time on the contract. In some ordinances, there are provisions to exempt contractors that are identified as facing extraordinary hardship under the ordinance. The combined effect of all of these exclusions and exemptions—particularly since the total employment of service contractors is small to begin with—means that in many cases very few workers are actually covered by the living wage.

In his review of living wage ordinances, Freeman notes "living wage campaigns pay a price for targeting small groups of workers in particular localities. The price is that the ordinances and policies affect only those relatively few workers. Most ordinances and policies cover at most a few hundred workers" (Freeman 2005).

These small numbers reflect what Jared Bernstein describes as the "paradox" of the living wage movement—activists succeed in passing ordinances, in part, by agreeing to narrow the focus and lower the cost of the ordinances (Bernstein 2005, 100). Ordinances are narrowed when exemptions are granted for particular types or sizes of contracts, broad classes of industries, and certain types of workers.[26]

[...]

Lessons for Policy Makers and Researchers

To date, most living wage research on which policy makers have had to rely has been prospective—they are written before the law has been implemented. With the increasing availability of quality studies and data on the actual (as opposed to projected) effects of living wages, future prospective studies should be less speculative and instead be based on the findings of the highest quality empirical studies.

Prospective studies have typically been created to inform and influence policy decisions, and have varied widely in their methodology, predictions, and accuracy. While a comprehensive review of prospective research is not within the scope of this paper, following are two predictions that prospective studies have commonly made, but have not been borne out.

Prediction one: significant costs to the municipality

Given sufficient information on the relevant contracts and workforce, it is possible to calculate reasonable estimates of the gross costs of mandated increases in wage and benefits from a living wage policy. It is more difficult, however, to determine who will ultimately pay for these cost increases. Prospective studies frequently focus on how much a living wage would cost the municipal government.

Lacking a significant body of research until recently, prospective studies have tended to base their predictions of how much of the cost pass-through would be passed onto local governments in the form of higher contract prices on educated speculation, sometimes justified with references to economic theory.

Some studies make the extreme assumption that local governments will absorb all of the cost increases from a living wage. Other studies, however, assume that governments will only absorb a portion of the cost increase, acknowledging that some of the costs will be offset through decreased turnover and increased productivity and that since costs from the living wage represent a very small portion of their overall cost of doing business, firms in a competitive bidding environment may ultimately pass little of the cost increase onto the municipal government.

Evidence from the retrospective studies suggests that this latter approach is probably the most realistic. In his review of the economic impacts of living wages, Brenner shows that studies predicting modest cost increases yielded estimates compatible with the effects measured by many retrospective studies (Brenner 2004, 38). Prospective studies produced by living wage opponents (e.g., Tolley 1999) have predicted massive costs that have not been reflected by the actual experience of cities. In many cases, studies have ignored factors that offset the costs, such as those described above.

Even cities budgeting for a new living wage policy have systematically overestimated the ultimate cost of the policy. Elmore's survey of cities that have enacted living wage laws shows that all of the cities that created budget forecasts significantly overestimated the actual costs of implementation. Actual costs ended up being between 30%-52% lower than what was forecast by the municipal government (Elmore 2003, 8).

To most accurately reflect the likely cost of the policy, prospective studies need to acknowledge, at bare minimum, that municipal governments will not bear all of the cost of a living wage, and most likely will experience only relatively small budget impacts.

Prediction two: significant employment losses

The economic impact of greatest interest for most prospective studies, and policy makers as well, is jobs. Most prospective studies have discussed potential impacts on employment and some have provided estimates of job loss. Typically these studies have relied on the minimum wage literature, both the theory and the empirical research, to infer the impacts of living wages on employment.

Some anti-living wage studies cite minimum wage research to support their claims of major job losses, but as esteemed labor economist Richard Freeman has concluded, the minimum wage "debate is over whether modest minimum wage increases have 'no' employment effect, modest positive effects, or small negative effects. It is not about whether or not there are large negative effects" (Freeman 1995, 833). This emerging consensus on the employment impacts of the minimum wage, however, is of limited use in the discussion of living wages because the living wage is set so much higher—anywhere between 50%–250% higher—than the federal minimum wage, with some living wage policies also requiring health insurance and other fringe benefits.

In addition, because the coverage of the two laws is so different, it is not clear they will have the same impacts on employment; while minimum wage laws cover most or essentially all firms in a geographic region, living wage ordinances cover the relatively few firms with direct voluntary financial relationships with municipal governments, and even then provide significant exemptions based on firm size and industry, as well as employee type. Given these differences of coverage and level of benefit, findings from the minimum wage literature cannot accurately translate to a living wage policy.

Conclusion

As in the debate over minimum wages, the question of the impacts of living wages on employment is ultimately answerable empirically. Thus far, the most reliable research on living wages suggests that the impact is modest. In the largest cities with the broadest-based living wage policies, there has been little measured employment loss. Given these results, prospective studies would do best to acknowledge that offsetting factors and modest costs for employers result in only limited job losses from a living wage policy. Ignoring the importance of offsetting factors will result in extreme overestimates of costs and job losses under a living wage policy.

Endnotes

9. The LAANE study used "needs-based" budgets developed by the California Budget Project and the National Economic Development and Law Center.

10. Although the survey was not based on a random sample, Brenner and Luce employed a variety of alternative sampling techniques to ensure that the surveyed workers are representative of the population of affected workers. See Brenner and Luce 2005, Appendix 6 for details.

11. Brenner and Luce 2005, tables 4.4 and 4.6.

12. Among the 76 "covered" workers with reliable before and after wage information, 32 earned below the living wage in 1998 and are considered "affected" workers.

13. Here "affected workers" are those in low-wage occupations who had been on the job between one and five years. The age of workers is their age when they started the job.

14. There was, however, a significant difference in reliance on part-time workers, with the share of part-time workers dropping considerably among affected firms.

15. The estimate of 1,000 workers getting a raise includes employees directly covered by the law, and the ripple effect on non-covered employees.

16. An estimated 1,850 workers who were already earning at or above the living wage level received indirect, or "spillover" raises. In his initial study, Fairris estimated 6,500 affected workers, but the figure was revised in later work he completed with LAANE.

17. An earlier version (Fairris 2005) reported larger, but still small, employment effects. The final version uses the same dataset, but with improved methodology.

18. Reich et al. demonstrate that this decline in airport traffic, which was also experienced by airports around the world, was due to a general decline in economic activity, and then to the events of September 11, 2001. Other Bay area airports fared better with airport traffic than SFO in 2001, primarily due to the relocation of Southwest Airlines to the Oakland airport, which left SFO after failing to secure additional terminal facilities (Reich 2005, 131-32).

19. Most of the studies also include other wage ranges as well and include the bottom quarter of workers, but the most consistent findings are for the lowest-wage 10% of workers. Also, the studies include specifications for contemporaneous effects, as well as

six- and 12-month lagged effects. The 12-month lagged effects are generally the most robust findings.

20. The Brenner, Wicks-Lim, and Polling figures are based on an assumption of 7,600 affected workers that was developed before the release of either the Fairris or LAANE studies.

21. There is disagreement between Neumark and Adams and their critics as to whether only one city in Neumark's 2002 study (as maintained by Brenner et al. 2002) had implemented the business assistance living wage provisions, or if the number is considerably larger. Whatever the exact number, it is certain that the actual impact of business assistance living wage ordinances is considerably less than an impression gained solely by looking at which cities had adopted these provisions in their city code. Neumark and Adams conduct interviews with municipal government administrators responsible for implementing the business assistance provisions of the living wage ordinance and reach a different conclusion than Brenner et al., finding that many cities are in fact implementing the provisions to some extent (Neumark and Adams 2005c, 19-20). As Bernstein points out, however, there is still a gap between what Neumark and Adams identify as "implemented" and what Brenner et al are implying in their critique: actually having to raise wages.

22. Brenner, Wicks-Lim, and Pollin indicate that Neumark's scheme covers 97% of workers, while Neumark (2002) identifies 90% of the bottom quartile of workers as being "covered."

23. Brenner et al. (2002) also make a technical point that by truncating his sample to focus on the lowest wage 10% of workers that Neumark could be introducing "sample selection bias." Instead, they argue that "quantile regression," focusing on the 10th percentile of the entire wage distribution is appropriate. Neumark and Adams respond that their truncation approach is necessary to capture the impacts of the living wage, and that, in fact, is unlikely to introduce sample selection bias. Neumark and Adams' argument on this point is probably correct, but is not relevant to the main part of the critique levied by Brenner et al.

24. Neumark and Adams claim not to understand this critique by Brenner et al, and do present a defense of their position. They do not, however, refute the Brenner et al. critique.

25. For an additional 10% of adopted ordinances, implementation has been blocked either by courts or elected officials, or was overturned by voters.

26. Nationwide there were potentially 100,000 workers that had received wage increases under living wage ordinances as of 2002, although dozens more successful campaigns since that time have likely increased that number by tens of thousands (Tanner 2002, 769).

References

Adams, Scott and David Neumark. 2005a. *A Decade of Living Wages: What Have We Learned?* San Francisco, Calif: Public Policy Institute of California.

Adams, Scott and David Neumark. 2005b. The economic effects of living wage laws: a provisional review. *Urban Affairs Review*. Vol. 40, No. 2, pp. 210-45.

Adams, Scott and David Neumark. 2005c. Living wage effects: new and improved evidence." *Economic Development Quarterly*. Vol. 19, No. 1, pp. 80-102.

Adams, Scott and David Neumark. 2004. When do living wages bite? *Industrial Relations*. Vol. 44, No. 1, pp. 164-92. Akerlof, George and Janet Yellen. 1990. The fair wage-effort hypothesis and unemployment. *Quarterly Journal of Economics*. Vol. 105, No.2, pp. 255-83.

Baiman, Ron, Joseph Persky, and Nicholas Brunick. 2002. *A Step in the Right Direction: An Analysis of the Forecasted Costs and Benefits of the Chicago Living Wage Ordinance*. Chicago, Ill.: Center for Urban Economic Development, University of Illinois, Chicago.

Bartik, Timothy. 2005. Thinking about local living wage requirements. *Urban Affairs Review*. Vol. 40, No. 2, pp. 269- 99.

Bernstein, Jared. 2005. "The Living Wage Movement: What Is It, Why Is It, and What's Known About Its Impact?" in Richard B. Freeman, Joni Hersch, and Lawrence Mishel, eds., *Emerging Labor Market Institutions for the Twenty- First Century*. Chicago, Ill.: The University of Chicago Press.

Bernstein, Jared and Jeff Chapman. 2002. *Time to Repair the Wage Floor: Raising the Minimum Wage to $6.65 Will Prevent Further Erosion of Its Value*. Washington, D.C.: Economic Policy Institute.

Bernstein, Jared, Chauna Brocht, and Maggie Spade-Aguilar. 2000. How Much is Enough? Basic Family Budgets for Working Families. Washington, D.C.: Economic Policy Institute.

Brenner, Mark D. 2004. The Economic Impact of Living Wage Ordinances. Working Paper No. 80. Amherst, Mass.: Political Economy Research Institute, University of Massachusetts, Amherst.

Brenner, Mark D. 2005. The economic impact of the Boston living wage ordinance. *Industrial Relations*. Vol. 44, No. 1, pp. 59-83.

Brenner, Mark D. and Stephanie Luce. 2005. *Living Wage Laws in Practice: The Boston, New Haven and Hartford Experiences*. Amherst, Mass.: Political Economy Research Institute.

Brenner, Mark, Jeannette Wicks-Lim, and Robert Pollin. 2002. Measuring the Impact of Living Wage Laws: A Critical Appraisal of David Neumark's How Living Wage Laws Affect Low Wage

Workers and Low-Income Families. Working Paper No. 43. Amherst, Mass.: Political Economy Research Institute.

Citro, Constance F. and Robert T. Michael, eds. 1995. *Measuring Poverty: A New Approach*. Washington, D.C.: National Academy Press.

Elmore, Andrew J. 2003. *Living Wage Laws & Communities: Smarter Economic Development, Lower than Expected Costs*. New York, N.Y.: Brennan Center for Justice.

Employment Policies Institute. 1998. *The Baltimore Living Wage Study: Omissions, Fabrications and Flaws*. Washington, D.C.: Employment Policies Institute.

Fairris, David. 2005. The impact of living wages on employers: a control group analysis of the Los Angeles ordinance. *Industrial Relations*. Vol. 44, No. 1, pp. 84-105.

Fairris, David and Michael Reich. 2005. The impacts of living wage policies: introduction to the special issue. *Industrial Relations*. Vol. 44, No. 1, pp. 1-13.

Fairris, David, David Runstein, Carolina Briones, and Jessica Goodheart. 2005. *The Los Angeles Living Wage Ordinance: Effects on Workers and Employers*. Los Angeles, Calif.: Los Angeles Alliance for a New Economy.

Freeman, Richard. 1995. What will a 10%...50%...100% increase in the minimum wage do? *Industrial & Labor Relations Review*. Vol. 48, No. 4, pp. 830-34.

Freeman, Richard. 2005. Fighting for other folks' wages: the logic and illogic of living wage campaigns. *Industrial Relations*. Vol. 44, No. 1, pp. 14-31.

Greenwald, Bruce and Joseph Stiglitz. 1988. "Pareto inefficiency of market economies: search and efficiency models. *American Economic Review*. Vol. 78, No. 2, pp. 351-55.

Howes, Candace. 2002. The Impact of a Large Wage Increase on the Workforce Stability of IHSS Home Care Workers in San Francisco County. Working Paper. New London, Conn.: Department of Economics, Connecticut College.

Howes, Candace. 2005. Living wages and retention of homecare workers in San Francisco. *Industrial Relations*. Vol. 44, No. 1, pp. 139-63.

Luce, Stephanie. 2005. The role of community involvement in implementing living wage ordinances. *Industrial Relations*. Vol. 44, No. 1, pp. 32-58.

Neumark, David and Scott Adams. 2000. Do Living Wage Ordinances Reduce Urban Poverty? Working Paper No. 7606. Cambridge, Mass.: National Bureau of Economic Research.

Neumark, David. 2002. *How Living Wage Laws Affect Low-Wage Workers and Low-Income Families*. San Francisco, Calif.: Public Policy Institute of California.

Niedt, Christopher, Greg Ruiters, Dana Wise, and Erica Schoenberger. 1999. The Effects of the Living Wage in Baltimore. Working Paper No. 199. Washington, D.C.: Economic Policy Institute.

Pollin, Robert. 2005. Evaluating living wage laws in the United States: good intentions an economic reality in conflict? *Economic Development Quarterly*. Vol. 19, No. 1, pp. 3-24.

Pollin, Robert. 2002. Santa Monica Living Wage Study: Response to Peer Reviews and Business Critics. Research Report No. 5. Amherst, Mass.: Political Economy Research Institute.

Preamble Center for Public Policy. 1998. *Baltimore's Living Wage: Response to Critics*. Washington, D.C.: Preamble Center for Public Policy.

Reich, Michael, Peter Hall, and Ken Jacobs. 2005. Living wage policies at the San Francisco airport: impacts on workers and businesses. *Industrial Relations*. Vol. 44, No. 1, pp. 106-38.

Reich, Michael, Peter Hall, and Ken Jacobs. 2003. *Living Wages and Economic Performance: The San Francisco Airport Model*. Berkeley, Calif.: Institute of Industrial Relations.

Reich, Michael, Peter Hall, and Fiona Hsu. 1999a. *Living Wages and the San Francisco Economy: The Benefits and the Costs* (First Release). Berkeley, Calif.: Bay Area Living Wage Research Group, Center on Pay and Inequality, Institute of Industrial Relations, University of California, Berkeley.

Reich, Michael and Peter Hall. 1999b. *Living Wages at the Airport and Port of San Francisco: The Benefits and the Costs*. Berkeley, Calif.: Bay Area Living Wage Research Group, Center on Pay and Inequality, Institute of Industrial Relations, University of California, Berkeley.

Reynolds, David and Jean Vortkamp. 2005. The effects of Detroit's living wage law on nonprofit organizations. *Economic Development Quarterly*. Vol. 19, No. 1, pp. 45-61.

Sander, Richard and Sean Lokey. 1998. *The Los Angeles Living Wage: The First Eighteen Months*. Norcross, Ga.: The Fair Housing Institute.

Tanner, Jane. 2005. Living wage movement: do laws requiring higher wages cause unemployment? *CQ Researcher*. Vol. 12, No. 33, pp. 769-92.

Tolley, George, Peter Bernstein, and Michael Lesage. 1999. *Economic Analysis of a Living Wage Ordinance*. Washington, D.C.: Employment Policies Institute.

Weisbrot, Mark and Michelle Sforza-Roderick. 1996. *Baltimore's Living Wage Law: An Analysis of the Fiscal and Economic Costs of Baltimore City Ordinance 442*. Washington, D.C.: Preamble Center for Public Policy.

Williams, Dana. 2004. Cleveland's Living Wage Law: A Three-Year Review. Cleveland, Ohio: Policy Matters Ohio. Williams, E. Douglas and Richard Sander. 1997. An Empirical Analysis of the Proposed Los Angeles Living Wage Ordinance: Final Report. http://www.law.ucla.edu/sander/L_Wage/Sander_LA-LivingWage-19970117.pdf.

11

A Living Wage Won't Hurt Employers

Results.org

Results.org is a non-profit movement of passionate, committed everyday people. Together they use their voices to influence political decisions that will bring an end to poverty.

Polling research shows that a significant number of Americans would like to see an increase in the minimum wage, and this valuable data should not go unnoticed. The Fair Minimum Wage Act of 2013 proposed that the minimum wage be raised in steps and indexed to the cost of living so that it does not lose value over time, and that gradual increase will prove beneficial to inflation rates while also pleasing U.S. workers.

Recent Developments

With the fourth anniversary of the last federal minimum wage increase to $7.25 an hour, the drum beat for increasing it is gaining strength. The President has asked for an increase as part of his economic recovery plan and polls of American citizens support it. The Fair Minimum Wage Act of 2013 has been introduced in Congress. There's a compelling reason driving this effort: the federal minimum wage has lost more than 30% of its value and would be more than $10.74 per hour today if it had kept pace with the cost of living over the past forty years.

In the President's 2013 State of the Union address, he called for raising the minimum wage. During the summer, he launched an economic recovery plan aimed at creating jobs and strengthening the middle class. In part of the plan, the President is calling on Congress to raise the minimum wage from $7.25 to $9 in stages by the end of 2015 and index it to inflation thereafter, which would directly boost wages for 15 million workers and reduce poverty and inequality.

This is what the American people want and would support. In a February 2013 poll conducted by Pew Research, 71 percent of Americans supported a federal minimum wage increase to $9.00 per hour, including 87 percent of Democrats, 68 percent of Independents, and 50 percent of Republicans. In an earlier 2012 poll by Lake Research Partners, nearly three-quarters of likely voters supported increasing the minimum wage to $10 and indexing it to inflation (73% support, 20% oppose) in 2014, including a solid 58% majority who felt that way strongly. Voters supported raising the minimum wage regardless of gender, age, education level, race, region, and partisanship. Intense support among Democrats (91% support overall and 79% strong support, 5% oppose) and Independents (74% support overall and 55% strong support, 18% oppose) was complemented by robust support from Republicans (50% support, 41% oppose) as well.

Senator Tom Harkin (D-IA), Chair of the Senate Health, Education, Labor and Pensions Committee, and Representative George Miller (D-CA), the top Democrat on the House Workforce Committee, have introduced The Fair Minimum Wage Act of 2013—S. 460 and H.R.1010. It would:

- Raise the federal minimum wage to $10.10 per hour by 2015, in three steps of 95 cents each.
- Adjust the minimum wage to keep pace with the rising cost of living starting in 2016—a key policy reform known as "indexing," which ten states are already using to prevent the minimum wage from falling in value each year.
- Raise the minimum wage for tipped workers—which has been frozen at a meager $2.13 per hour for more than twenty years—to 70% of the full minimum wage.

Background and History

"It is but equity...that they who feed, clothe and lodge the whole body of the people, should have such a share of the produce of their own labor as to be themselves tolerably well fed, clothed and lodged."-Adam Smith, The Wealth of Nations, 1776

The federal minimum wage was signed into law in 1938 by President Franklin Roosevelt, at the height of the Great Depression. Its purpose was to keep America's workers out of poverty, and increase consumer purchasing power in order to stimulate the economy.

The current federal minimum wage has been $7.25 since 2009. This level was embedded in an emergency war funding bill signed by President Bush in 2007, following a period of ten years when the level had not been adjusted. The bill put in place a three-level wage increase that went from $5.15 an hour to $5.85 in 2007, to $6.55 in 2008, and to $7.25 since July 24, 2009.

An individual working full time at $7.25 an hour would earn $15,080 a year. On that salary there is no state where a worker—for example, a single working mother—could afford a two-bedroom apartment. For more facts about the minimum wage, see the National Employment Law Project's "Raise the Minimum Wage" campaign pages.

In addition, more families than ever are relying on low-wage and minimum wage jobs to make ends meet. Many jobs lost during the recession were in higher-wage sectors like construction, manufacturing and finance. But 58 percent of all jobs created in the post-recession were low-wage occupations, according to a 2012 report by the National Employment Law Project. This is not a short term trend—six of the top ten growth occupations projected by the U.S. Bureau of Labor Statistics for next decade are low-wage jobs, including home health aides, customer service representatives, food preparation and service workers, personal and home care aides, retail salespersons, and office clerks. Raising the minimum wage would boost pay scales in these types of jobs where millions of Americans today spend their careers.

Has the minimum wage kept up with inflation? Hardly. This graph reveals the sad facts which most Americans know from their daily lives and those of relatives and friends who have suffered from the recession and not yet recovered. The recession severely worsened what was already a decades-long diminishment of the buying power of the minimum wage. The federal minimum wage has lost more than 30% of its value and would be more than $10.74 per hour today if it had kept pace with the cost of living over the past forty years.

Reasons to Increase the Minimum Wage

Raising the wage level to the $10.10 level would help 30 million working Americans and their families make a decent living. Those people are not teenagers—88% are adults over the age of 20, 56% are women, nearly half are workers of color, and over 43% have some college education. More than 17 million children have a parent who would get a raise under the bill introduced. See more analysis of Census data by the Economic Policy Institute. The median worker age is close to 40 for home health care workers, one of the nation's top-growth low-wage occupations. Especially after the recession, more and more Americans are spending their careers in low-wage jobs where the minimum wage helps set pay scales.

As people's wages rise, it follows that their need in accessing safety net programs like the Supplemental Nutrition Assistance Program or SNAP, or low-income housing would diminish. By keeping the minimum wage low, businesses have increased the need for government support systems. It's time for businesses to pay a living wage again that is part of a healthy economy, especially since research is clearly showing that a higher minimum wage would not impact job creation.

Raising the minimum wage right now in a sluggish economy is more important than ever. Minimum wage increases stimulate the economy by increasing consumer spending, without adding to state and federal budget deficits. Consumer spending drives 70 percent of the economy, and increasing demand is key for jumpstarting production and creating more jobs. Yet wages and salaries now make up the lowest share of national income since 1966, while corporate profits are now the largest share of national income since 1950. The Economic Policy Institute estimates that The Fair Minimum Wage Act of 2013 would generate more than $32 billion in new economic activity, translating to 140,000 new full-time jobs as higher sales lead businesses to hire more employees.

"The biggest problem Main Street businesses face is lack of customer demand," says Holly Sklar, director of the Boston-based Business for Shared Prosperity, a network of progressive business owners and investors. "With the federal minimum wage stuck … workers now have less buying power than they did a half century ago in 1956, and far less than they had at the minimum wage's $10.55 high point in 1968, adjusted for inflation. We can't build a strong economy on downwardly mobile wages. It's time to raise America by raising the minimum wage."

An increase in the minimum wage is supported by both Republican and Democrat business leaders. Two out of three small business owners (67%) support increasing the federal minimum wage and adjusting it yearly to keep up with the cost of living. The strong support for a minimum wage raise is particularly striking since the small business owners are predominately Republican. The poll was conducted March 4-10, 2013 by Greenberg Quinlan Rosner Research on behalf of Small Business Majority. View the poll findings summary. The poll shows 65% of small business owners agree that "increasing the minimum wage will help the economy because the people with the lowest incomes are the most likely to spend any pay increases buying necessities they could not afford before, which will boost sales at businesses. This will increase the customer demand that businesses need to retain or hire more employees."

> *"Paying your employees well is not only the right thing to do but it makes for good business."-Jim Sinegal, CEO, Costco*

Common Myths and Objections from the National Employment Law Project (NELP)

Raising the minimum wage causes job loss.

Not true. The best economic research, and real world experiences with minimum wage increases, confirms that raising the minimum wage does not cause job loss. The decade following the federal minimum wage increase in 1996-1997 ushered in one of the strongest periods of job growth in decades. Analyses of states with minimum wages higher than the federal floor between 1998 and 2003 showed that their job growth was actually stronger overall than in states that kept the lower federal level. The most sophisticated minimum wage study to date, published in November 2010 by economists at the University of Massachusetts, University of North Carolina, and University of California, compared employment data among every pair of neighboring U.S. counties that straddle a state border and had differing minimum wage levels at any time between 1990 and 2006, and found that minimum wage increases did not cost jobs. A companion study published in April 2011 found that these results hold true even during periods of recession and high unemployment.

Raising the minimum wage hurts teenage workers.

Not true. A recent rigorous study by economists at the University of California examining the impact of minimum wage increases on teen unemployment found that even minimum wage increases implemented during times of high unemployment—such as the recessions of 1990-1991, 2001 and 2007-2009—did not result in job losses for teens or slow employment growth.

Critics like to suggest that the last increase in the federal minimum wage in 2009 caused a spike in teen unemployment. But as a NELP report demonstrated in 2011, teen unemployment rises faster than adult joblessness during every recession—whether or not the minimum wage goes up. This is because teens are the last hired, and so are always the first fired when the economy shrinks and adults compete with them for scarce jobs.

Employers may go out of business if they have to pay a higher minimum wage.
Not true. While opponents frequently make this claim, research and experience demonstrate otherwise. In fact, many of the loudest minimum wage opponents are the country's largest and most profitable companies. A 2012 report by NELP found that two-thirds of all low-wage workers are employed by large companies rather than small businesses, and that the vast majority of the largest low-wage employers in the country are earning strong profits and can afford higher wages.

It's also important to remember that since the minimum wage has lost so much value over the last several decades, employers today are actually being allowed to pay less—in real dollars—than they were in the late 1960's.

State Efforts

Nineteen states, including the District of Columbia, have raised their minimum wage above the level set by federal law. The state of Washington has the highest state minimum wage at $9.19 (with the future level indexed to inflation). Oregon follows closely behind at $8.95 (also indexed). Ten of the 19 states have also linked their state minimum wage to the consumer price index, so that the rate automatically keeps pace with inflation each year (AZ, CO, FL, MO, MT, NV, OH, OR, VT, and WA). For more information, see the map at the Center for Economic and Policy Research.

Legislation to raise and/or index the minimum wage has been introduced in several states. In some of those states, activists are organizing campaigns to support the increase. In other states, the minimum wage has come under attack and worker justice advocates are fighting back. Read more to see what's going on in your state or to discover that your state needs action to raise the minimum wage!

12

The Working Poor Deserve a Living Wage

Carla A. Katz, Esq.

Carla A. Katz is an assistant teaching professor at Rutgers School of Management and Labor Relations at Rutgers University. She is also an attorney with the law firm of Cohen, Placitella, Roth, PC.

Families relying on low wages are forced to make choices between things like paying for food, rent, or electricity and keeping their children clothed and in school—and when the federal minimum wage was introduced, it was intended to help those families earn a decent living. Unfortunately, research reveals that those standards have not kept up with inflation. Many voters, even in politically conservative states, have expressed a desire to raise the minimum wage to fix that inequality in the system.

A noxious combination of falling wages, income inequality at its highest since the 1920s and a growing low-wage sector has caused the ranks of the working poor to swell to more than 47 million. That's one out of every seven Americans.

Harnessing the anger and economic pain that workers are feeling at the decimation of the middle class, a living wage movement made up of grassroots groups, unions and community organizations has been pushing hard to reverse that trend on numerous front, including by lifting minimum pay at all levels of government. The activists are targeting a US$15 hourly rate in the retail and fast food sectors and trying to pass living wage resolutions that aim to increase base salaries above the poverty line.

While activists have yet to reach their goals at the federal level, they have been very successful convincing voters in cities and states—both conservatives and liberals—to raise their own minimums closer to a living wage. As more states and cities raise their minimums in a significant way, pressure rises on Congress to pass an increase of the federal minimum wage rate. Workers also are making demands directly of their employers, including a visible campaign among fast food and retail workers demanding higher wages, regular schedules, full-time work and dignity on the job.

Voters Want Wage Hikes

Most Americans support an increase because long-term economic pain has become excruciating for so many. Voters have come to see it and the accompanying income inequality as issues that affect them.

How else to explain why 66% of voters in politically conservative Arkansas, home to Walmart, the country's largest employer, chose to raise the minimum wage? Prior to the midterm elections, the wage was US $6.25 (one dollar below the federal minimum). Now it will rise to US $8.50 by 2017.

Businesses that directly or indirectly depend on low wages increasingly understand that treating employees well means they will treat customers well. About 62% of employers surveyed earlier this year on behalf of CareerBuilder.com believe that the minimum wage should rise.

Workers' Woes Resonating

One reason the struggles of low-wage workers are resonating with Americans is that so many newly created jobs pay very little. According to a study by the National Employment Law Project, 44% of employment growth in the last four years has been in low-wage jobs. Middle-income positions are being steadily replaced by jobs paying less than $10 an hour. Worse, involuntary part-time work has pulled 7 million Americans into poverty or near it.

While efforts by President Obama and Democrats in Congress to raise the federal minimum wage to $10.10 withered in Washington this summer, the midterm elections highlighted the strong bipartisan public support for giving it a much-needed boost.

In an overwhelmingly Republican state, a whopping 69% of voters in Alaska endorsed [increasing theirs] to $9.75 by 2016 from $7.75 today. Nebraska followed suit with 59% approving a $1.75 bump to $9 by 2016. In South Dakota, 55% voted to raise the minimum wage $1.25 to $8.50.

By January, 29 of 50 states (and the District of Columbia) will boast minimum wages higher than the federal rate. Additionally, more than 130 cities have enacted legislation or resolutions to restore a strong wage floor. Voters in Seattle and San Francisco have led the way with $15 hourly minimums.

Many cities have also enacted "living wage laws" that establish a higher minimum wage for employers that receive contracts or subsidies from local government. Workers also are making demands directly of their employers, including a campaign among fast-food and retail workers demanding higher wages, regular schedules, full-time work and dignity on the job.

Fast Food on the Front Lines

That fast food and retail workers occupy the front lines of the living wage fight makes sense since the industries employ about two thirds of low-wage workers. The top 12 US companies paying workers the least are national restaurant chains such as McDonalds, Starbucks and Taco Bell and retailers like Walmart, Target and Sears.

Walmart, which earned more than $16 billion last year, cost American taxpayers $7.8 billion in subsidies and tax breaks, while the majority of their employees earned less than $25,000 a year.

Below the Poverty Line

The federal minimum wage has risen occasionally since 1938 from 25 cents an hour to its current level of $7.25, where it has remained since 2009. In the 1960s, the minimum wage was equal to roughly half the national average but today it is worth only 37%. Minimum wage workers employed full-time earn just $15,000 a year, falling under the poverty line for a family of two.

If the 1968 minimum wage had kept pace with inflation, it would be $10.90 today. A 2012 study by the Center for Economic and Policy Research noted that if the minimum wage had kept pace with productivity, it would be $21.72 an hour, and if it had kept pace with the wage growth of the wealthiest 1%, it would be $29 an hour.

Moving the Economy Forward

Raising the federal minimum wage is not enough to reduce the inequality gap that is causing Americans so much pain. We need more jobs that pay a living wage so a family can afford basic needs such as food, adequate shelter and the ability to deal with emergencies and other necessities of life.

When he introduced the federal minimum wage in 1933, President Franklin D Roosevelt said, "No business which depends for existence on paying less than living wages to its workers has any right to continue in this country. By living wages, I mean more than a bare subsistence level. I mean the wages of a decent living."

Too many working families are making impossible choices— between paying for food or rent or electricity. A vital US economy that works for all of us needs a thriving middle class. For that to be realized, good jobs—full time with a fair wage that lets families live a comfortable life—must be the norm. The recent ballot box victories and continuing protests across the country prove that Americans understand their collective power to turn the tide.

13

Higher Minimum Wage Alone Won't Solve Poverty

T.H. Gindling

Tim Gindling is Professor of Economics and Director of the graduate program at University of Maryland, Baltimore County (UMBC).

Studies show that minimum wage laws in developing countries have limited effects on reducing poverty. Additionally, many low-wage earners are informal workers and therefore not covered by the laws. There are many pros and cons in this debate, but one thing is clear: For minimum wage increases to have any meaningful impact on global poverty rates, they must be combined with other safety net programs targeted at low-income families and low-skill job markets.

Elevator Pitch

Raising the minimum wage in developing countries could increase or decrease poverty, depending on labor market characteristics. Minimum wages target formal sector workers—a minority in most developing countries—many of whom do not live in poor households. Whether raising minimum wages reduces poverty depends not only on whether formal sector workers lose jobs as a result, but also on whether low-wage workers live in poor households, how widely minimum wages are enforced, how minimum wages affect informal workers, and whether social safety nets are in place.

"Does increasing the minimum wage reduce poverty in developing countries?" by T. H. Gindling, IZA. Article Reprinted with Permission, IZA world of labour (wol.iza.org).

More than half of workers in developing countries are not covered by minimum wage legislation

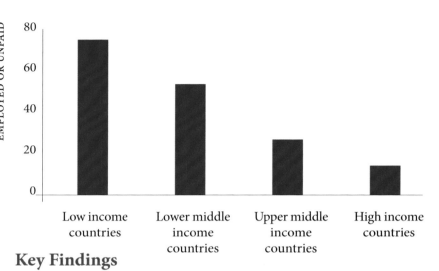

Key Findings

Pros

- If job losses in the formal sector are small, raising the minimum wage is likely to reduce poverty.
- If informal sector wages rise when the minimum wage increases, higher minimum wages are likely to reduce poverty.
- If the people earning the minimum wage are heads of low-income households, higher minimum wages are likely to reduce poverty.
- If low-income workers lose jobs and cannot find jobs because of a higher minimum wage, social safety nets for low-income households can protect against poverty.

Cons

- If higher minimum wages cause workers to lose formal sector jobs, they are not likely to reduce poverty.

- If minimum wage legislation does not cover a large pool of informal workers, higher minimum wages are not likely to reduce poverty.
- If the people on the minimum wage are secondary family workers, higher minimum wages will not reduce poverty.
- If low-income workers lose jobs and cannot find jobs because of higher minimum wages and there are no social safety nets, higher minimum wages will increase poverty.

Author's Main Message

Raising the minimum wage reduces poverty in most developing countries. But the impact is modest because the legal minimum wage applies to only a minority of poor workers; in particular, it does not cover workers in the large informal sector. And raising the minimum wage creates losers as well as winners among poor households—depending on employment effects, wage distribution, and effects on the household head—pulling some out of poverty while pushing others in. Raising the minimum wage could be part of a comprehensive poverty-reduction package but should not be the only, or even the main, tool to reduce poverty.

Motivation

A popular and compelling argument in favor of raising legal minimum wages is that higher minimum wages will reduce poverty. Quite simply: putting more money into the pockets of low-income workers will allow them to purchase more of the basic goods and services needed to survive. In theory, if the wage increase is large enough, poor people's incomes will rise, lifting them out of poverty.

This sounds good in theory—but it does not always happen in practice. That is because the relationship between minimum wages, worker incomes, and employment levels, and the incidence and depth of poverty are complex.

First, the minimum wage does not affect all workers or affect them equally. That makes it important to know which workers are most likely to be affected—and how. Second, even if a minimum wage raises the incomes of some workers, it might not raise the incomes of poor households. The informal sector, where workers are not effectively covered by minimum wage legislation, is typically large in developing countries, and poverty tends to be more widespread in the informal sector. Even in the formal sector, minimum wage laws are often poorly enforced.

There are also employment effects to consider. An increase in the minimum wage may cause some employers to lay off workers. If these workers live in low-income households, poverty may increase, at least in the short term. Layoffs may also put downward pressure on wages in both the formal and informal sectors.

For all these reasons, increasing the minimum wage might have no positive impact on poverty—or worse, might backfire and deepen poverty, especially for the extremely poor.

Discussion of Pros and Cons

Impacts on wages and employment in the formal sector influence the effect on poverty

Minimum wage increases most directly affect earnings and employment in the formal sector. Higher minimum wages lead to higher wages for the formal sector workers who keep their jobs. Studies for developing countries, mostly in Latin America, suggest that the positive wage effect is strongest for workers earning near the minimum wage. As a result, increases in the minimum wage tend to compress the wage distribution (equalize wages) in the formal sector.

Increases in the minimum wage might not help formal workers most in need. Some workers affected by the minimum wage increase already earn above the old minimum wage. In Latin America the minimum wage is often used as a guide by employers in setting all wages, even those well above the minimum wage.

In addition, minimum wages might affect the wages of high-wage workers because some countries have multiple minimum wages. In Costa Rica, where wages are set by occupation and skill, a university graduate being paid the minimum wage for that category of worker would be in the top 10% of the wage distribution.

All these effects are for workers who retain their jobs. What about employment? The evidence is mixed. The majority of studies conclude that increasing the minimum wage reduces formal employment, although the effect appears to be small in most countries. Almost all estimates suggest that a 1% increase in the minimum wage results in less than a 1% decrease in employment, implying that the total earnings of formal sector workers increase when minimum wages rise.

Impacts on wages and employment in the informal sector also influence the effect on poverty

The impact of the minimum wage on wages and employment—and poverty—also depends on what happens in the informal sector. More than half of workers in low- and lower-middle-income countries work in this sector, which is not covered by minimum wage legislation (see Figure 1). This complicates the picture. A large informal sector can cushion the effect on poverty of a higher minimum wage if workers who lose jobs or who cannot find formal sector jobs as a result of the increase find work in the informal sector—even low wages are better than no wages. But the effect could be just the opposite for some workers. Higher minimum wages might force more workers out of the formal sector and into the informal sector, and the lower wages could push their households below the poverty line.

In some countries, higher minimum wages have resulted in higher wages for workers in both the formal and informal sectors (some researchers call this the "lighthouse effect"). In other countries, higher minimum wages seem to have little or no impact on wages in the informal sector. No study has found that a higher minimum wage depresses wages for informal sector workers as a whole.

Taken together, the evidence for developing countries suggests that a higher minimum wage generally leads to an increase in

Composition of workforce by income group

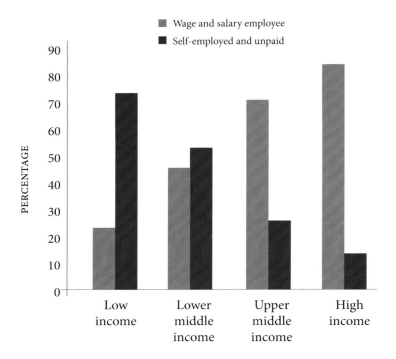

total earnings for workers as a group. However, the evidence also suggests that a higher minimum wage creates both winners and losers. Some workers see their earnings increase, while others see their earnings fall because they become unemployed, leave the labor force, or are forced into lower-paid jobs in the informal sector.

How do these wage and employment dynamics in the formal and informal sectors affect poverty? It is not possible to know based on aggregate wage and employment data alone. The key issue is how households are affected by the minimum wage. Even if raising the minimum wage increases total earnings for workers, higher minimum wages could still increase poverty if the benefits go to workers who are not poor and the costs are paid by workers who are.

Impacts can vary along the wage distribution

Understanding the impact of minimum wages on poverty requires understanding their impact at different points in the wage distribution. For policymakers, that issue can affect how the minimum wage is set and with what wage group in mind.

For example, when minimum wages are low relative to average wages (as in Brazil and Mexico), they tend to raise the wages of workers at the bottom of the wage distribution. But when minimum wages are high relative to average wages (as in Colombia), they will increase the wages of workers in the middle but not at the bottom of the wage distribution.

Thus higher minimum wages will only affect those whose wages are high relative to average wages (since those earning less than the minimum wage are not directly affected by minimum wages). While the benefits of higher minimum wages are distributed across the wage and skill distribution, studies in developing countries suggest that employment losses tend to be concentrated among workers with characteristics associated with low wages.

Negative effects on employment can also vary along the wage distribution. Overall, women, young workers, and less-educated workers, whose wages tend to be low, suffer the heaviest employment losses. In Brazil, Colombia, and Costa Rica, employment losses were largest at the bottom of the distribution of wages and skills, though there were sometimes smaller employment losses even for workers earning well above the minimum wage.

Do workers affected by minimum wages live in poor households?

Factoring in the wage distribution can increase understanding of how minimum wages might affect poverty. But it is still necessary to know the household income of workers at different wage levels, because poverty is defined in terms of household income, not individual earnings.

For example, a worker in the upper half of the wage distribution might live in a poor household, so a higher minimum wage could help that worker's household escape poverty. Or a worker at the bottom of the wage distribution could be a secondary wage earner in a nonpoor household, so a higher minimum wage would make this household better off but would not reduce poverty.

The impact of higher minimum wages on poverty also depends on whether the concern is solely with the number of households with incomes below the poverty line (the incidence of poverty) or also with how far the poor are below the poverty line (the poverty gap). In the second case, it will matter which poor households benefit and which poor households lose when minimum wages rise. Raising the minimum wage could raise the incomes of some poor households with incomes near the poverty line while reducing the incomes of the poorest households at the bottom of the distribution (Figure 2).

Fig. 2: Minimum wage relative to the household per capita proverty lines

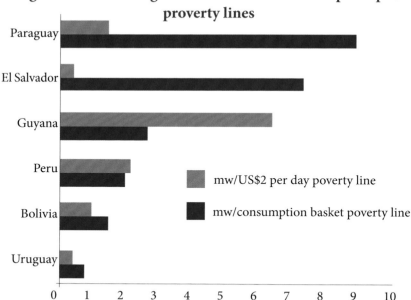

Studies using aggregate country-level data to examine the correlations between minimum wages and poverty have generally found that in developing countries higher minimum wages are correlated with lower poverty rates. However, this research also suggests that minimum wages do not affect the poorest share of the population but rather the upper levels of the low-income population, those with incomes near the poverty line.

A few studies use individual- or household-level data to examine the impact of higher minimum wages across the household income distribution. The findings suggest that higher minimum wages modestly reduce poverty rates.

- In Mexico, workers in the poorest households had the largest wage gains following an increase in the minimum wage (reducing the poverty gap), but the wage gains were not large enough to push most of these households above the poverty line.
- In Colombia, workers earning the minimum wage were most likely to be in households in the middle of the income distribution (see Figure 3); the poorest households did not benefit from minimum wages.
- Likewise, in Brazil, higher minimum wages did not raise the incomes of households in the bottom three deciles of the household income distribution.

Fig. 3: Workers in Colombia earning minimum wage were most likely in the middle of the income distribution

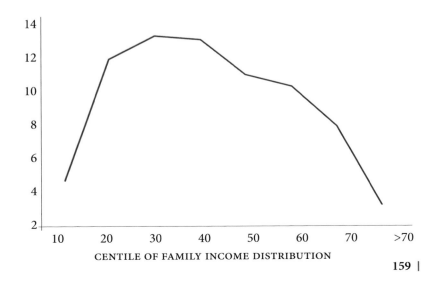

CENTILE OF FAMILY INCOME DISTRIBUTION

This suggests that higher minimum wages in Colombia and Brazil did lead to moderate declines in poverty overall but did not reduce poverty among the very poorest households. In other words, minimum wages modestly reduced the incidence of poverty but increased the gap between the average incomes of the poorest households and the poverty line.

Impacts may differ between household members

The impact of minimum wages on household incomes also depends on how many household members are working and how each worker is affected by minimum wages.

For example, higher minimum wages will not affect the incomes of households in which no one is working. In low-income households with more than one worker, raising the minimum wage could increase the earnings of one household member and reduce the earnings of another. If the workers earning the minimum wage are secondary workers in households whose total income is well above the poverty line, a higher minimum wage will have little or no impact on poverty. But it is also possible that a higher minimum wage could induce secondary family workers in poor households to work more, boosting household incomes.

Whether minimum wages are more likely to affect household heads or secondary family workers is particularly important. For example, in Honduras, where multiple minimum wages mean that one worker in the household could face a higher minimum wage than another, higher minimum wages only reduce household poverty if the minimum wage affects the household head.

Results from studies in Brazil, Colombia, and Nicaragua suggest that if a higher minimum wage increases the wages of household heads without leading to large employment losses, poverty will fall (this will happen even if secondary workers lose work). On the other hand, if minimum wages have a significant negative employment effect on household heads, then higher minimum wages will have, at their best, only modest impacts on poverty (this will happen even if there are positive employment effects on secondary family workers).

In Colombia, higher minimum wages had a significant negative effect on the employment and hours worked of household heads, but not on the employment and hours worked of secondary workers. In Brazil, higher minimum wages also reduced the employment of household heads and increased labor force participation slightly for other household members. As noted, higher minimum wages in Colombia and Brazil had a modest impact on poverty and no impact on the incomes of the poorest households.

But in Nicaragua the reverse holds: household heads were less likely than other members to lose their jobs because of higher minimum wages. Moreover, household heads who lost their jobs because of higher minimum wages were more likely to find work in the public sector or as self-employed workers, while other household members who lost their jobs were more likely to leave the labor force. As a result, higher minimum wages caused a statistically significant and substantial reduction in poverty in Nicaragua.

In summary, if minimum wages have a positive wage effect but a small negative employment effect on household heads, then higher minimum wages are more likely to reduce poverty (even if there are significantly negative employment effects on non-household heads). On the other hand, if minimum wages have a significantly negative employment effect on household heads, then higher minimum wages are less likely to reduce poverty (even if there are positive employment effects on secondary family workers).

Impacts of higher minimum wages on nonlabor income
Minimum wages can also affect other sources of income received by poor households. For example, social safety net programs can soften the negative impacts of higher minimum wages on poor households by supplementing incomes when a household member loses a job.

Several Latin American countries tie many of the social benefits for low-income households to the minimum wage. In Brazil, for example, where noncontributory pensions make up a large portion of the income of many poor households and their value is tied to the minimum wage, higher minimum wages substantially lowered poverty between 1994 and 2004. The higher minimum wages were responsible for 32% of the unprecedented reduction in income inequality in Brazil in the 1990s and 2000s because of their impact on nonlabor incomes.

One danger of tying social safety net payments or eligibility to the minimum wage is that higher minimum wages may strain government budgets, forcing curtailments of public spending on other important government priorities.

In addition, the minimum wage is generally not a good proxy for the subsistence needs of households; for half the countries in Latin America, it is insufficient to provide for household needs. The best practice is usually to anchor social assistance to a given consumption bundle or to economy-wide average earnings.

Income transfers between households may also be important. In South Africa and some other developing countries, income is shared among households to ease the impact of a negative shock. A higher degree of income sharing between the employed and unemployed reduces the probability that a higher minimum wage will push a household into poverty.

Limitations and Gaps

The research on the wage and employment impacts of minimum wages in developing countries is voluminous, but most of it concerns Latin American countries; other regions have been studied much less. And, even in Latin America, there is little research on other factors that affect the relationship between minimum wages and poverty. Among the most important information gaps in most countries is how and why raising the minimum wage affects household members in different ways—and whether the impacts differ in poor and nonpoor households.

For most countries, it would be useful to determine whether workers who earn the minimum wage are likely to live in poor households and whether they are likely to be household heads or secondary family workers. More difficult, but also quite important, would be to estimate the positive wage effects and negative employment impacts of minimum wages separately for different household members, especially for household heads and secondary workers and for households in different parts of the income distribution.

Summary and Policy Advice

Most empirical studies of the impact of minimum wages on poverty in developing countries conclude that increases in minimum wages reduce poverty, on balance, though they find only a modest impact—for two reasons.

- First, a large share of workers is not covered by minimum wage legislation.
- And second, higher minimum wages do not affect all low-income households the same way: minimum wages pull some households out of poverty, but may push others into poverty.

Given the potential for negative impacts on the employment status and incomes of some of the poorest families, raising minimum wages is an inefficient tool for reducing poverty. More efficient policies would focus on

- enhancing compliance with minimum wage laws,
- improving incomes in the informal sector where minimum wages do not apply, and
- increasing the long-term productivity of workers from low-income families.

This suggests that while minimum wages can be part of a package of poverty-reducing policies, they should not be the only mechanism or even the most important one.

For example, Brazil's conditional cash transfer program, Bolsa Familia, was more effective than higher minimum wages at reducing poverty and income inequality using an identical amount of resources. Conditional cash transfers to low-income households have the additional benefit of providing part of a social safety net for households when workers lose their jobs because of higher minimum wages. Labor supply incentives, particularly the earned income tax credit, have also been shown to be effective in increasing both the employment and earnings of low-income workers in the US.

14

Minimum Wages Aren't a Free Lunch

David Neumark

David Neumark is professor of economics and director of the Center for Economics and Public Policy at the University of California, Irvine.

When enacted, minimum wage policies involve several trade-offs that the casual observer may not be aware of. While some families may see benefits from higher wages, evidence from many countries around the world suggests that employment opportunities are reduced overall. Research indicates that enacting minimum wage laws creates both "winners" and "losers" in the job market and may have unintended consequences for the very people the laws are designed to help.

Elevator Pitch

The potential benefits of higher minimum wages come from the higher wages for affected workers, some of whom are in poor or low-income families. The potential downside is that a higher minimum wage may discourage employers from using the low-wage, low-skill workers that minimum wages are intended to help. If minimum wages reduce employment of low-skill workers, then minimum wages are not a "free lunch" with which to help poor and low-income families, but instead pose a tradeoff of benefits for some versus costs for others. Research findings are not unanimous, but evidence from many countries suggests that minimum wages reduce the jobs available to low-skill workers.

"Employment effects of minimum wages," by David Neumark, IZA. Article reproduced with permission of IZA world of labour (wol.iza.org).

Key Findings

Pros

- Many low-wage, low-skill workers retain their jobs and earn higher wages when minimum wages are increased.
- Some studies do not find that minimum wages lead to fewer jobs.
- Living wage policies, adopted by some municipalities in the US, may help reduce poverty.
- Targeted tax credits do a better job of reaching the poor than minimum wages do.

Cons

- Compelling evidence from many countries indicates that higher minimum wage levels lead to fewer jobs.
- Studies that focus on the least-skilled workers find the strongest evidence that minimum wages reduce jobs.
- Low-paying jobs requiring low skills are the jobs most likely to decline with increased minimum wages.
- In the US, higher minimum wages do not help poor or low-income families.

Author's Main Message

Although a minimum wage policy is intended to ensure a minimal standard of living, unintended consequences undermine its effectiveness. Widespread evidence indicates that minimum wage increases are offset by job destruction. Furthermore, the evidence on distributional effects, though limited, does not point to favorable outcomes, although some groups may benefit.

Motivation

The main case for a minimum wage is that it helps poor and low-income families earn enough income. However, the potential downside is that it may discourage employers from using low-wage, low-skill workers. If minimum wages destroy jobs for low-skill workers, that creates winners and losers. Whether a minimum wage reduces poverty or helps low-income families then depends on where along the distribution of family incomes these winners and losers are located. Clearly, the effect on jobs is critical: If a higher minimum wage does not destroy jobs, then from the government's perspective it is a free lunch that helps reduce poverty, even if higher-income families also benefit. Labor economists have long studied whether minimum wages destroy jobs. This paper looks at the accumulated evidence, and also at the reliability of the underlying research methods for estimating the effects of the minimum wage on jobs.

Discussion of Pros and Cons

Theory

Textbook analyses of minimum wages portray a competitive labor market for a single type of labor, with an upward-sloping labor supply curve (S) and a downward-sloping labor demand curve (D). With no minimum wage, there is an equilibrium wage, w, and an equilibrium quantity of labor employed, L (see Figure 1).

With a "binding" minimum wage mw that is higher than w, fewer workers are employed, for two reasons. First, employers substitute away from the now more expensive labor and toward other inputs (such as capital). Second, because costs are higher with this new input mix, product prices rise, which further reduces labor demand. These two effects lead to lower employment

Of course this model oversimplifies. One issue is that workers have varying skill levels, and minimum wages are unlikely to matter for higher-skill workers. Employers will substitute away from less-skilled workers toward more-skilled workers after a minimum wage increase. This "labor–labor" substitution has implications for empirical evidence on the employment effects of minimum wages. The employment declines might not appear to be large, even if the disemployment effect among the least-skilled workers is strong.

This is relevant from a policy perspective. The minimum wage is intended to help the least-skilled workers. If their employment declines substantially, the policy is self-defeating.

A more fundamental challenge to the competitive model is that it is simply the wrong model. Some argue that there can be "monopsony" in labor markets, because of frictions that tie workers to specific firms. These frictions imply that when an employer hires another worker, the cost of existing workers also increases. As a consequence, market determined employment can fall below the economically efficient competitive level. Moreover, in this model, a minimum wage can sometimes lead to higher employment.

Evidence

Economists describe the effect of minimum wages using the employment elasticity, which is the ratio of the percentage change in employment to the percentage change in the legislated minimum wage. For example, a 10% increase in the minimum wage reduces employment of the affected group by 1% when the elasticity is −0.1 and by 3% when it is −0.3.

Through the 1970s, many early studies of the employment effects of minimum wages focused on the US. These studies estimated the effects of changes in the national minimum wage on the aggregate employment of young people, typically 16–19-yearolds or 16–24-year-olds, many of whom have low skills. The consensus of these first generation studies was that the elasticities for teen employment clustered between −0.1 and −0.3 [1].

Limited evidence from the 1990s challenged this early consensus, suggesting that employment elasticities for teenagers and young adults were closer to zero. But even newer research, using more up-to-date methods for analyzing aggregate data, found stronger evidence of disemployment effects that was consistent with the earlier consensus. Using data through 1999, the best of these studies found teen employment elasticities of −0.12 in the short run and −0.27 in the longer run, thus apparently confirming the earlier consensus: Minimum wages destroy the jobs of young (and hence unskilled) people, and the elasticity ranges between −0.1 and −0.3.

In the early 1990s, a second, more convincing wave of research began to exploit emerging variation in minimum wages across states within the US. Such variation provides more reliable evidence because states that increased their minimum wages can be compared with states that did not, which can help account for changes in youth employment occurring for reasons other than an increase in the minimum wage. A related literature focuses on specific cases of state minimum wages increases. This case study approach offers the advantage of limiting the analysis to a state where the minimum wage increases and another very similar state that is a reasonable comparator. Unfortunately, these results do not necessarily apply in other states and other times.

An extensive review of this newer wave of evidence looked at more than 100 studies of the employment effects of minimum wages, assessing the quality of each study and focusing on those that are most reliable [2], [3]. Studies focusing on the least skilled were highlighted, as the predicted job destruction effects of minimum wages were expected to be more evident in those studies. Reflecting the greater variety of methods and sources of variation in minimum wage effects used since 1982, this review documents a wider range of estimates of the employment effects of the minimum wage than does the review of the first wave of studies [1].

Nearly two-thirds of the studies reviewed estimated that the minimum wage had negative (although not always statistically significant) effects on employment. Only eight found positive employment effects. Of the 33 studies judged the most credible, 28, or 85%, pointed to negative employment effects. These included research on Canada, Colombia, Costa Rica, Mexico, Portugal, the UK, and the US. In particular, the studies focusing on the least-skilled workers find stronger evidence of disemployment effects, with effects near or larger than the consensus range in the US data. In contrast, few—if any—studies provide convincing evidence of positive employment effects of minimum wages.

One potential exception is an investigation of New Jersey's 1992 minimum wage increase that surveyed fast-food restaurants in February 1992, roughly two months before an April 1992 increase, and then again in November, about seven months after the increase [4]. As a control group, restaurants were surveyed in eastern Pennsylvania, where the minimum wage did not change. This allowed comparing employment changes between stores in New Jersey and Pennsylvania. The results consistently implied that New Jersey's minimum wage increase raised employment (as measured by full-time equivalents, or FTEs) in that state. The study constructed a wage gap measure equal to the difference between the initial starting wage and the new minimum wage for fast-food restaurants in New Jersey and equal to zero for those in Pennsylvania. The increase had a positive and statistically significant effect on employment growth in New Jersey (as measured by FTEs), with an estimated elasticity of 0.73. Note that the study did not, as is often claimed, find "no effect" of a higher minimum, but rather a very large positive effect.

A reassessment of this evidence looked at the unusually high degree of volatility in the employment changes found in the data [5]. The new study collected administrative payroll records from fast-food establishments in the same areas from which the initial study had drawn its sample. In the initial survey, managers or assistant managers were simply asked, "How many full-time and part-time workers are employed in your restaurant, excluding managers and assistant managers?" [4]. This question is highly ambiguous, as it possibly refers to the current shift, the day, or the payroll period. In contrast, the administrative payroll data clearly referred to the payroll period. Reflecting this problem, the initial survey data indicated far greater variability than the payroll records did, with some implausible changes.

When the minimum wage effect was re-estimated with the payroll data, the minimum wage increase in New Jersey led to a decline in employment in New Jersey relative to employment in Pennsylvania [5]. The estimated elasticities ranged from

−0.1 to −0.25, with many of the estimates statistically significant. In response to these results, the authors of the original study used data from the US Bureau of Labor Statistics on fast-food restaurant employment, this time finding small and statistically insignificant effects of the increase in New Jersey's minimum wage on employment.

By far the largest number of studies use US data because state-level variation provides the best "laboratory" for estimating minimum wage effects. Many studies focus on the UK, which enacted a national minimum wage in 1999. A national minimum wage poses greater challenges to social scientists, because it is difficult to define what would have happened in the absence of a minimum wage increase. This challenge is reflected in the UK studies. Absent variation in minimum wages across regions in the UK, one recent study examines groups differentially affected by the national minimum wage, finding employment declines for part-time female workers, the most strongly affected. A second study looks at changes in labor market outcomes at ages when the UK minimum wage changes—at 18 and 22—and finds a negative effect at age 18 and at age 21 (a year before the minimum wage increases, which the authors suggest could reflect employers anticipating the higher minimum wage at age 22). However, there are numerous UK studies that do not find disemployment effects.

The current summary differs from many other brief synopses of minimum wage studies, which often point out that some studies find negative effects and others do not. The studies reporting positive or no effects are often given too much weight. Studies suggesting that "we just don't know" often summarize the literature by citing one or two studies finding positive effects, such as [4], along with a couple of studies reporting negative effects, suggesting that one should not confidently hold the view that minimum wages reduce employment. However, the piles of evidence do not stack up evenly: The pile of studies finding disemployment effects is much taller.

The large review of minimum wage studies also highlights some important considerations when assessing the evidence on minimum wages [2]. First, case-study analyses may cover too little time to capture the longer-run effects of minimum wage changes. Second, case studies focusing on a narrow industry are hard to interpret, since the standard competitive model does not predict that employment will fall in every narrow industry or subindustry when an economy-wide minimum wage goes up.

This view of the overall lessons to be drawn from the large body of research on minimum wages has been contested in a review from 2013 [6], drawing in part on previous metaanalysis. The review uses the estimates displayed in Figure 1 in that meta-analysis to suggest that the best estimates are clustered near zero. However, the figure includes a pronounced vertical line at a zero minimum wage-employment elasticity, creating the illusion that the estimates are centered on zero. This illusion is perhaps further enhanced by including studies with elasticities ranging from nearly −20 (that is, 100 times larger than a −0.2 elasticity) to 5, making it hard to discern whether the graph's central tendency is closer to 0, −0.1, or −0.2, which is the relevant debate. In fact, the previous meta-analysis reports that the mean across the studies summarized in the graph is −0.19.

Moreover, applying meta-analysis to minimum wage research is problematic. Metaanalysis treats all studies as equally valid, aggregating them to estimate an overall effect. This approach is intuitively appealing for combining estimates from similar experiments that differ mainly in the samples studied, because it turns many small samples into one large one. However, combining minimum wage studies without taking into account the variations in the reliability of their methods and in the groups of workers studied compromises the findings of such meta-analysis.

Two recent revisionist studies find no detectable employment losses from US minimum wage increases [7], [8]. These studies argue that higher minimum wages were adopted in states where the employment of teenagers and other low-skill workers was declining because of deteriorating economic conditions generally, so the negative relationship does not necessarily imply a negative causal effect.

More convincingly, another study suggests that when economic conditions are considered, minimum wage policies have an even stronger effect in reducing employment [9]. That study looks at variations in state minimum wages that arise not from the decisions of state legislators, who could be responding to immediate economic conditions, but from national decisions, which are less likely to respond to state-level economic conditions. The study finds evidence that teenage employment is negatively affected by minimum wage increases, with elasticities as large as −1, although smaller in some cases. This evidence suggests stronger disemployment effects of minimum wages than most other studies find.

Moreover, a review of the two studies finding no detectable employment losses finds that their conclusions are not supported by the data. The review suggests that the data show elasticities nearer to −0.15 for teenagers and some signs of negative employment effects for restaurant workers, although other factors make this hard to estimate [10]. The review concludes that elasticities of employment for groups strongly affected by minimum wage policies are in the range found by many earlier researchers, from −0.1 to −0.2.

Estimates in this range suggest that for groups of workers strongly affected by the minimum wage, disemployment effects are relatively modest. That has led some people to conclude that there are, at most, "small" disemployment effects. However, these elasticities understate the effects on the most affected workers, because even among these groups many workers earn more than the minimum wage. Suppose, for example, that half of teenagers earn the minimum wage and that a rise in the minimum wage sweeps them from the old minimum to the new one. And suppose that the other half of teenagers earn above the new minimum wage and are not affected by the increase. Then, a 10% increase in the minimum wage with a −0.15 elasticity for teens implies that teen employment will decline 1.5%. However, this decline occurs solely among the teenagers earning below the new minimum wage. Since in this example they make up just half of teenagers, their employment must fall 3% to generate a 1.5% decline among all teenagers.

Distributional effects—In brief

The main argument proffered in favor of a minimum wage is that it helps poor and low-income families. But because there are some disemployment effects, minimum wages create winners and losers. The winners get a higher wage with no reduction inemployment (or hours), while the losers bear the burden of the disemployment effects—losing their job, having their hours reduced, or finding it more difficult to get a job. If the gains to the winners are large, if these winners are disproportionately from the low-income families that policymakers would like to help, and if the losses are concentrated among higher-income workers or other groups from whom policymakers are willing to redistribute income, then the losses experienced by the losers from a minimum wage increase may be deemed acceptable. However, research for the US fails to find evidence that minimum wages help the poor; they may actually increase the number of poor and low-income families.

The fundamental problem with using minimum wages to increase the incomes of poor and low-income families is that the policy targets low-wage workers, not low-income families, which are not necessarily the same. Consider the US federal minimum wage of $7.25 an hour in 2008. Although 13.2% of people lived in poor households in 2008, only 4.4% of all workers lived in poor households.

Moreover, many minimum wage workers lived in non-poor and even relatively high-income households. Only 12.7% of workers earning a wage of less than $7.25 an hour were in poor households, while 44.6%—or nearly half, most of whom were probably teenagers or other secondary workers—were in households with incomes three times the poverty line (or approximately $63,000 in 2008 for a family of four) or higher. Thus, if the benefits of the minimum wage were spread equally across all affected low-wage workers, only 12.7% of the benefits would go to poor households, and nearly half would go to households in the top half of the household income distribution.

Another reason minimum wages may fail to help low-income families is that many low-income families have no workers. Of families whose head was below age 65 in 2010, 52% of families below the poverty line had no labor income, while only 6% of families above the poverty line had none.

If the winners from a minimum wage increase are low-wage workers in poor families, and the losers are low-wage workers in high-income families, minimum wages would redistribute income to poor families. But the opposite is also plausible. A comprehensive study covering state and federal minimum wage increases between 1986 and 1995 (welfare reforms in 1996 could confound analyses using data after 1995) finds that minimum wage increases do not reduce the number of poor families and may even increase it slightly [12]. The results are similar for families below 1.5 times the poverty line, sometimes referred to as a marker of near-poverty. Other studies reach similar conclusions. In short, there is no compelling evidence of beneficial distributional effects of minimum wages in the US.

The distributional effects of minimum wages could well vary with other factors, however, such as institutions and policies or features of the wage and income distribution that influence the targeting of minimum wages. Research shows that living wages— wage floors adopted by some US cities that target city contractors or businesses that receive financial assistance from cities—also generate job losses but do a better job of targeting benefits to poor families. The broader, financial-assistance versions of these laws generate modest reductions in urban poverty. Most of the research is based on experiences in the US, although there is evidence that minimum wages in Brazil did not generate beneficial distributional effects. US results may not apply elsewhere.

The inability to help poor and low-income families through a higher minimum wage is understandably frustrating for policymakers. In the US, however, a far more effective policy tool is the Earned Income Tax Credit (EITC) enacted in the 1970s. Some European countries have implemented similar policies. These programs pay subsidies to lowincome workers, based on family income; the subsidies are phased out as income rises.

While the incentive effects of these subsidies are often complicated, the subsidies, handled correctly, unambiguously create an incentive to enter the labor market for eligible individuals who were not working. Moreover, the subsidies depend on family income, thus creating incentives precisely for the families most in need of help. Poverty rates are very high for female-headed families with children, for example, and there is overwhelming evidence of the EITC's positive employment effects for single mothers. Moreover, the EITC helps families escape poverty not simply through the EITC subsidy, but also through the added labor market earnings generated because of the labor supply incentive effects of the EITC [13].

Combining the EITC with a higher minimum wage can lead to better distributional effects than the minimum wage alone, although it increases the adverse effects of the minimum wage on other groups [13]. That is because a higher minimum wage coupled with an EITC can induce more people who are eligible for the EITC to enter the labor market, while exposing people who are not eligible for the EITC to greater competition in the labor market, which can amplify the disemployment effects for them. An exploration of the interactions between higher state minimum wages in the US and the more generous state EITC programs finds that a combination of the two policies leads to more adverse employment effects on specific groups—like teenagers and less-skilled minority men—that are not eligible for the EITC (or are eligible for a trivial credit), while finding positive employment and distributional effects for single women with children who are eligible. This research does not change the conclusion that minimum wages destroy jobs; rather, it shows that the effects can vary across subpopulations—in this case because of interactions with another policy.

Limitations and Gaps

There are two key gaps in our understanding of the effects of a minimum wage. One concerns the interactions between minimum wages and other labor market institutions and policies and the ultimate disemployment effects. This question has been explored for countries within the Organisation for Economic Co-operation and Development (OECD), but the analysis needs to be extended to developing countries as well, where the policy variation is greater.

The other concerns how minimum wages affect different groups and regions. For example, it would be helpful to be able to isolate the employment effects of minimum wages on poor, low-income, and other families to find out whether the negative effects are concentrated on low-wage workers in low-income families. If so, this would add to the weight of the evidence against higher minimum wages. If not, the fairly modest disemployment effects would need to be reconciled with no apparent beneficial distributional effects.

Summary and Policy Advice

While low wages contribute to the dire economic straits of many poor and low-income families, the argument that a higher minimum wage is an effective way to improve their economic circumstances is not supported by the evidence.

First, a higher minimum wage discourages employers from using the very low-wage, low-skill workers that minimum wages are intended to help. A large body of evidence confirms that minimum wages reduce employment among low-wage, low-skill workers.

Second, minimum wages do a bad job of targeting poor and low-income families. Minimum wage laws mandate high wages for low-wage workers rather than higher earnings for low-income families. Low-income families need help to overcome poverty. Research for the US generally fails to find evidence that minimum wages help the poor, although some subgroups may be helped when minimum wages are combined with a subsidy program, like a targeted tax credit.

The minimum wage is ineffective at achieving the goal of helping poor and low-income families. More effective are policies that increase the incentives for members of poor and low-income families to work.

Footnotes

[1] Brown, C., C. Gilroy, and A. Kohen. "The effect of the minimum wage on employment and unemployment." *Journal of Economic Literature* 20:2 (1982): 487–528.

[2] Neumark, D., and W. Wascher. "Minimum wages and employment." *Foundations and Trends in Microeconomics* 3:1–2 (2007): 1–186.

[3] Neumark, D., and W. Wascher. *Minimum Wages.* Cambridge, MA: MIT Press, 2008.

[4] Card, D., and A. B. Krueger. "Minimum wages and employment: A case study of the fast-food industry in New Jersey and Pennsylvania." *American Economic Review* 84:5 (1994): 772–793.

[5] Neumark, D., and W. Wascher. "Minimum wages and employment: A case study of the fastfood industry in New Jersey and Pennsylvania: Comment." *American Economic Review* 90:5 (2000): 1362–1396.

[6] Schmitt, J. Why Does the Minimum Wage Have No Discernible Effect on Employment? CEPR Discussion Paper, 2013.

[7] Dube, A., T. W. Lester, and M. Reich. "Minimum wage effects across state borders: Estimates using contiguous counties." *Review of Economics and Statistics* 92:4 (2010): 945–964.

[8] Allegretto, S. A., A. Dube, and M. Reich. "Do minimum wages really reduce teen employment? Accounting for heterogeneity and selectivity in state panel data." *Industrial Relations* 50:2 (2011): 205–240.

[9] Baskaya, Y. S., and Y. Rubinstein. Using Federal Minimum Wage Effects to Identify the Impact of Minimum Wages on Employment and Earnings across US States. Unpublished Paper, Central Bank of Turkey, 2011.

[10] Neumark, D., J. M. I. Salas, and W. Wascher. "Revisiting the minimum wage–employment debate: Throwing out the baby with the bathwater?" *Industrial and Labor Relations Review* 67:3(2014): 608–648.

[11] Sabia, J. J., and R. V. Burkhauser. "Minimum wages and poverty: Will a $9.50 federal minimum wage really help the working poor?" *Southern Economic Journal* 76:3 (2010): 592–623.

[12] Neumark, D., M. Schweitzer, and W. Wascher. "The effects of minimum wages on the distribution of family incomes: A non-parametric analysis." *Journal of Human Resources* 40:4 (2005): 867–917.

[13] Neumark, D., and W. L. Wascher. "Does a higher minimum wage enhance the effectiveness of the Earned Income Tax Credit?" *Industrial and Labor Relations Review* 64:4 (2011): 712–746.

15

Companies Around the World Must Act Now to Raise Minimum Wage

Rachel Wilshaw

Rachel Wilshaw is the ethical trade manager for Oxfam GB. Oxfam is an international confederation dedicated to fighting poverty.

Since we live in an increasingly global economy, goods and products are manufactured and sold in many parts of the world by workers at varying levels of pay. Low-wage jobs often exist within a company's supply chain. In many countries, minimum wages are seen as being the market wage as opposed to being a floor wage, and those wages often fall short of the cost of living for families.

Almost a century after the ILO Constitution recognized the need for workers to earn a living wage, the question of whether wages enable workers to meet their needs and those of their families has gained renewed momentum. Much has been written on the issue, but very little that assesses how companies are implementing it, and the outcomes.

In this paper, we outline the root causes of low wages, the barriers to ensuring a living wage is paid and the compelling reasons for responsible companies to act now. We give credit for steps taken in a range of sectors, provide a framework for deeper change and signpost initiatives that are aligned with this. The

Adapted from publisher from *Steps Towards A Living Wage In Global Supply Chains*, 2014 with the permission of Oxfam, Oxfam House, John Smith Drive, Cowley, Oxford OX4 2JY UK www.oxfam.org.uk. Oxfam does not necessarily endorse any text or activities that accompany the materials, nor has it approved the adapted text.

aim is to help companies who source from developing countries understand and tackle the issue and see what success looks like from an Oxfam perspective.

The Issue of a Living Wage

Over the last 25 years, income from labour has made up a declining share of GDP across low-, middle- and high-income countries alike.[2] As Oxfam highlighted in its 2014 report 'Even It Up: Time to End Extreme Inequality', this is a key driver of growing inequality which is harmful both for society and the economy.[3]

A living wage[4] does more than keep people out of poverty. It allows them to participate in social and cultural life and afford a basic lifestyle considered acceptable by society at its current level of development.[5] It is a human right.[6] When a profitable company does not ensure a living wage is paid, it is pushing onto the most vulnerable people in its supply chain the negative impact of its business model. This is unfair and unsustainable.

Living Wage and the UN Guiding Principles

'Business needs to demonstrate it contributes to the common good. The living wage is one of the most powerful tools for business to contribute to their workers' human rights.' --Phil Bloomer, Executive Director, Business & Human Rights Resource Centre.[10]

The UN Guiding Principles on Business and Human Rights set out companies' responsibility to respect human rights, including in their business relationships in the supply chain. They must identify adverse human rights impacts and address them, even if they have not contributed to those impacts. Adverse impacts clearly include forced and child labour, such as that found in cotton, seafood and palm oil.[11] But they also include the millions of 'low road' jobs—many of them legal—in which workers cannot work their way out of poverty, however hard they try.[12] Job insecurity is as much part of the problem as low wages[13] and women are on a 'lower road' than men.[14] It is part of due diligence that sourcing companies assess the number of workers on 'low road' jobs in their supply chain and set them on a rising path.

What Is Driving Low Wages?

In Oxfam's analysis, there are three key drivers of low wages in global supply chains:

1. Unfair share of value in the chain

Business models push cost and risk down the supply chain to maximise profit for shareholders. There is a disconnect between corporate responsibility programmes and sourcing strategies.

Wages of garment workers have fallen in real terms, but prices paid have not increased. A survey by Fair Wage Network[19] found workers commonly rely on overtime, yet 68 percent of Asian garment suppliers reported difficulty paying overtime premiums.

Executive pay, though, continues to rise. Every CEO in the UK's top companies takes home £4.25 million a year on average, nearly double their income in 2002. This is 131 times as much as their average employee[20] and around 2,000 times as much as a typical garment worker in Bangladesh.[21]

2. Absence of collective bargaining

A major barrier to higher wages is the absence of collective bargaining. Trade unions are a vital countervailing force to capital that helps ensure prosperity is shared. Yet companies often treat trade unions as adversaries rather than as partners. Women make up a large part of the workforce in global supply chains, but most are unaware of their rights and have little or no voice in the workplace. They also carry a much greater care burden that restricts their ability to organise.

Denmark has no minimum-wage law, but $20 an hour is the lowest the fast-food industry can pay under a collective bargaining agreement between 3F union and an employers' group which includes Burger King and McDonald's. In the United States fast-food workers, serving the same companies' products but unable to bargain collectively, earn an average of just $8.90.[22]

3. Inadequate minimum wage

Minimum wages fall short of the cost of living in many countries as governments compete for investment in a global market. The minimum wage is seen as the 'going rate' rather than a floor. Corporate lobbying often reinforces the message that business wants light touch regulation.[23]

Some governments have bucked the trend. Brazil's minimum wage rose 50 percent in real terms from 1995 to 2011, and poverty and inequality declined in step. China has pursued a deliberate policy of raising wages since the 2008 economic downturn.[24]

Forces for and Against Taking Action

Oxfam recognizes that a company cannot 'just pay a living wage' along its supply chain. In many cases it is not the legal employer; the first or second tier supplier is. Wage levels and enforcement depend on the political, social and economic context. If a sourcing company pays more, there is no guarantee the extra money will reach the workers. Employers fear becoming less competitive, buyers fear falling foul of competition law. But there are also compelling reasons to take action.

Steps in the Right Direction

Progressive corporate codes, such as the Ethical Trading Initiative (ETI) Base Code and SA8000, incorporated a living wage in the late 1990s. However, it has taken many years for companies to give serious consideration to payment of a living wage in their own operation and supply chains. While progress was made in health and safety[26] which is less challenging, and child labour, which carries reputational risks, it is only with the increasing momentum of living wage campaigns in recent years that practical steps are starting to be taken.

- In 2009 the grassroots-based Asia Floor Wage campaign took the debate up a level by setting out to dismantle companies' arguments for not implementing a living wage. A group of Asian unions and non-government organizations (NGOs) proposed a formula approach, based on atypical number of earners and dependents, and published benchmarks for Asian countries covering 80 percent of global garment production. Clean Clothes Campaign and Label Behind the Label reinforced the case for action by publishing assessments of brands' performance, most recently Tailored Wages which covers 50 brands and coincided with the first anniversary of the collapse of Rana Plaza.[27]
- Early steps in the right direction were taken by Inditex, which signed an International Framework Agreement with the garment union in 2007 (re-affirmed in 2014) and Marks & Spencer which included in its 2010 corporate plan a commitment to pay a price that enabled a 'fair living wage' to be paid in Bangladesh, India and Sri Lanka.
- Programmes were initiated to improve human resource management and increase productivity, enabling wages to be increased with minimal impact on the bottom line. Impactt's Benefits for Business and Workers programme, set out with eight brands and 73 factories supplying them, to develop a virtuous circle of improvements. It reports that worker turnover reduced by 50 percent in Bangladesh and 25 percent in India, an additional $6.6m was added to workers' wages over a 12 months period[28] and in Bangladesh, 43 percent fewer workers worked more than 60 hours a week. Employers received a good return on their investment.

"We have been able to increase our knitting workers' incomes by one third...Workers can go home on time and spend evenings and weekends with their families. Our workers stay with us for longer and have better skills."—Director of Operations, RMG factory, Bangladesh[29]

- Switcher worked with a factory in Bangladesh to establish a wage fund for workers; Nudie Jeans did something similar in India. Tchibo has sponsored training of worker representatives. GAP has committed to raise the wage floor of its employees in the USA to $10 in 2015.
- Many of these brands are members of ETI which has reinforced its expectations of corporate members on implementing a living wage, provided guidance and a seven step guide to approaching the issue, and initiated workshops and tripartite communities of practice (companies, NGOs, trade unions) to enable sharing of practical experience.
- In the food sector, Unilever replaced its traditional supplier code with a Responsible Sourcing Policy based on a continuous improvement framework covering mandatory requirements, good practice and best practice standards. It has published targets for 200 'Partner to Win' suppliers and 1,000 strategic partners (11,200 sites in all) to achieve 'good practice' standards by 2017; these include a 'living wage approach to fair compensation'. Nestlé became the first major food manufacturer in the UK to become an accredited Living Wage employer in 2014.
- Certification: In 2013 six members of ISEAL Alliance agreed jointly to commission living wage benchmarking studies from experts Richard and Martha Anker.[30] Utz Certified has incorporated a living wage into its code. Of the certification bodies, Fair Trade has done most to make its commitment to living wage explicit by strengthening its Hired Labour Standard, adopting a Freedom of Association protocol to remove barriers to worker organizing and requiring that wages be negotiated with workers and rise more than inflation.
- In the electronics industry, Fairphone has built better wages into its business model, with consumers and the manufacturer in China, Guohong, each contributing $2.50 for each phone sold. Consulted on the first bonus, a workers' welfare committee chose a wage supplement and subsidized meals.

- In furniture, IKEA worked with Fair Wage Network on an assessment of its retail units in four countries against the '12 dimensions of a fair wage.'[31] It is now working to close the gaps identified. In Japan it has closed a significant wage and benefits gap between full-time retail workers and part-timers (mostly women). In China, where excessive working hours is the norm, it has worked with suppliers to reduce hours without a reduction in wages. In the USA it has raised its wage floor to $10.76 an hour.

Investing in Deeper Change

These initiatives represent steps in the right direction, but in terms of results, very little has changed for very few workers. To achieve a tipping point, a more systemic approach is needed. This goes beyond increasing value for wages and leads towards governments having inclusive minimum wage-setting processes, employers who have bought into the agenda and have the capacity and flexibility to deliver it, and workers being able to negotiate terms.

Stakeholder collaboration in the banana industry

Since 2010, the World Banana Forum has enabled multi-stakeholder dialogue on issues facing the industry, with support from the FAO. Unlike many cross-industry initiatives, it involves trade unions, small producer organizations and southern governments actively in the process. Severe supermarket competition in Europe has made the commercial context even more challenging.[32] Yet forum members continue to work on living wage and 'cost of sustainable production' issues.

A forum working group on distribution of value, which includes major supermarkets, is exploring ways to increase the price paid to producers to cover the 'cost of sustainable production' and ensure the additional value reaches workers. Following dialogue within the forum, the Ecuador government committed to raising the national minimum wage by more than inflation and eliminating labour sub-contracting so workers are covered by social security.'[33]

In Cameroon, a joint platform led by local trade unions and IUF, supported by Fairtrade International and BananaLink has negotiated wage increases and abolished the lowest wage grades. In 2014, the Government of Cameroon raised the national minimum wage in the agriculture sector for the first time in many years.[34]

In 2013 supermarket giant Tesco, as a result of the work of the World Banana Forum, committed to pay banana prices that at least covered the Fairtrade minimum price, and in November 2014 became the first retailer to announce that it would pay a living wage to banana workers in key sourcing sites by 2017.[35]

Stakeholder collaboration in the tea industry

In the tea sector, Oxfam has continued to work alongside the Ethical Tea Partnership, since our joint report, to find sustainable ways to improve wages on Malawi's tea estates. As wages are set at national and not at tea estate level, this has required development of a sector wide programme involving the supply chain from producers to retailers, including the Tea Association of Malawi, certification organisations Fairtrade, Rainforest Alliance and UTZ Certified, development partners IDH and GIZ with international wage expertise from Richard and Martha Anker and Ergon Associates. Fairtrade and the Tea Association of Malawi also commissioned a study by Imani Development estimating the price of tea needed to sustain a Living Wage.

The programme seeks to improve tea productivity and quality and strengthen human resource management, linked to a commitment to raise wages. It includes tackling barriers to worker representation and collective bargaining and looking into ways to improve nutrition and banking facilities for workers.[36]

Moving 'beyond audit' in the garment industry

Multi-stakeholder initiative Fairwear Foundation (FWF) has taken a range of approaches to nudge corporate members 'beyond audit' and to remove barriers to a living wage. It has developed Wage Ladders (which include benchmarks from local trade unions) which help members set improvement targets, and instituted a Performance Benchmarking System which rewards action and penalizes inaction. The system looks at pricing, sourcing from locations where the company has leverage and long-term relationships and advocacy to governments.

FWF has taken a methodical approach to analysing obstacles. With brands specializing in outdoor wear, and using hypothetical products (to meet competition law), it found that because supply chain actors calculate their fees as a multiple of the 'FOB' price, a rise in wages which would add $3 to the product cost would mean $18 was added to the retail price.[37]

FWF also uses complaints as catalysts for positive change, for instance in Turkey where 38 complained of being dismissed from a knitwear factory and were protesting outside the factory. Relationships between the owners and the union were strained but FWF and the brand sourcing there—Mayerline—encouraged dialogue and the dispute was resolved. The employer has since become the first knitwear factory in Turkey to negotiate a Collective Bargaining Agreement, which covers wages (now close to a living wage), social benefits and working hours.[38]

Fair Wage Network has conducted Fair Wage assessments, using management and worker surveys and surveys of workers' expenditure, that highlight the value of working in partnership with companies. Assessments have been carried out for brands including Puma in Indonesia, Adidas in the Philippines and H&M in several countries. Discussion has moved on from changes needed at factory level (e.g. pay systems, overtime, wage levels) to ways of scaling up the improvements.

H&M showed it has grasped the need for a more holistic approach in its Roadmap to a Living Wage, which highlights the roles of governments, trade unions and employers as well as stating its willingness 'to pay more so that our suppliers can pay higher wages'.

Change catalysed by Rana Plaza

The Accord on Fire and Building Safety in Bangladesh, brokered by UNI Global Union and IndustriALL, has shown it is possible to change how brands operate. Its immediate focus is building safety following the collapse of Rana Plaza, but includes provision for fair prices as well as worker participation. Five new collective bargaining agreements have been finalized and the minimum wage has been increased, though its purchasing power is only a fifth of that in China.

Fourteen corporate members of the Bangladesh Accord have signed up to four enabling principles for a living wage:

1. Enabling employees' freedom of association and collective bargaining;
2. Working on wage systems that reward skill and productivity;
3. Adjusting purchasing practices in line with wage policies;
4. Influencing governments.

In September 2014 following months of unrest eight brands wrote an open letter to the Cambodian government and industry association stating their readiness to factor higher wages into their pricing.[40] In November the government raised the minimum wage by 28 percent.

London Citizens and Living Wage Employers in the UK

The Living Wage Campaign was started in 2001 by parents in the East End of London, whose long working hours on the minimum wage meant they had little time to spend with their families. The national wage of £7.85 (21 percent above the national minimum wage of £6.50), is calculated and updated annually by the Centre for Research in Social Policy at Loughborough University. In order to lead promote this the Living Wage Foundation was set up in 2010 as a project of Citizens UK.

In 2011 only two of the top 100 UK companies were living wage employers; now there are 19, with 10 more in the pipeline and over 1000 accredited employers in total, including Oxfam GB. The campaign's momentum has been helped by high profile champions, broad political support and an annual Living Wage Week which celebrates success and calls for more. Accredited employers report benefits in terms of productivity, staff turnover and motivation as well as reputation.[41] While the numbers benefitting are still relatively small—60,000 against over five million paid below the living wage—the initiative has helped normalize discussions in the business community and provides a 'bridgehead of principle' to action in global supply chains.

Endnotes

1. http://www.labourbehindthelabel.org/staff/item/1179-new-research-shows-clothing-factory-workers-seriously-malnourished

2. J.Ghosh (2013), 'A Brief Empirical Note of the Recent Behaviour of Factor Shares in National Income, *Global & Local Economic Review*, 17(1), p.146, http://gler.it/archivio/ISSUE/gler_17_1.pdf.

3. http://policy-practice.oxfam.org.uk/publications/even-it-up-time-to-end-extreme-inequality-333012

4. Oxfam defines a living wage as 'one which for a full-time working week (without overtime) would be enough for a family to meet its basic needs and allow a small amount for discretionary spending'. Offside! *Labour Rights and Sportswear Production in Asia*, Oxfam.

5. http://www.fairtrade.net/fileadmin/user_upload/content/2009/resources/LivingWageReport_ExecutiveSummary_Malawi.pdf

6. United Nations Universal Declaration of Human Rights, Article 23 (3).

7. See Further Reading section on p.14

8. Working poor in America http://www.oxfamamerica.org/explore/research-publications/working-poor-in-america/

9. http://www.behindthebrands.org/en/company-scorecard. The campaign was voted runner-up in the UK Sustainability Leader Awards in November 2014 for its public engagement on sustainability issues.

10. Email exchange with the author, November 2014.

11. http://www.theguardian.com/global-development/2014/jun/10/supermarket-prawns-thailand-produced-slave-labour; http://www.somo.nl/publications-en/Publication_4110; http://www.businessweek.com/articles/2013-07-18/indonesias-palm-oil-industry-rife-with-human-rights-abuses.

12. International Trade Union Congress (2014), 'Frontlines Report', ITUC, http://www.ituc-csi.org/frontlines-report-february-2014-14549?lang=en

13. http://wiego.org/publications/contract-labour-global-garment-supply-chains

14. http://www.capturingthegains.org/pdf/GVC_Gender_Report_web.pdf

15. Collective bargaining assumes freedom of association is in place where legally mandated. Freedom of association and the right to collective bargaining are fundamental rights underpinning all other labour rights. See http://www.ethicaltrade.org/resources/key-eti-resources/freedom-of-association-in-company-supply-chains for a guide for companies.

16. http://www.labourbehindthelabel.org/news/item/1179-new-research-shows-clothing-factory-workers-seriously-malnourished

17. Labour behind the Label, 'Shop till they drop', http://www.labourbehindthelabel.org/news/item/1195-shoptildrop

18. http://www.waronwant.org/campaigns/living-wage/17978-report-the-living-wage; 'Lessons for social change in the global economy'; The right to organise, living wage and real change for garment workers Sarah Adler-Milstein, Jessica Champagne and Theresa Haas (Garwood)

19. https://www.northumbria.ac.uk/static/5007/despdf/designres/dougproject.pdf

20. http://highpaycentre.org/blog/ftse-100-bosses-now-paid-an-average-143-times-as-much-as-their-employees

21. Calculation is based on a number of variables and assumes Bangladesh garment worker earns minimum wage 5300 Tk per month for 12 months plus average 22 per cent overtime (based on http://capturingthegains.org study), with both incomes adjusted for $ Purchasing Power Parity (based on http://worldbank.org/indicator).

22. http://www.nytimes.com/2014/10/28/business/international/living-wages-served-in-denmark-fast-food-restaurants.html?_r=0

23. http://www.stern.nyu.edu/experience-stern/about/departments-centers-initiatives/centers-of-research/business-human-rights/activities/supply-chains-sourcing-after-rana-plaza

24. Oxfam 'Even it Up!' report, op cit, page 78.

25. http://www.fairtrade.net/single-view+M5fc5b408f70.html—_ftn1

26. http://www.ethicaltrade.org/resources/key-eti-resources/eti-impact-assessment-report-summary

27. http://www.labourbehindthelabel.org/campaigns/itemlist/category/295-tailored-wages

28. http://www.impacttlimited.com/wp-content/uploads/2013/10/BBW-Nicer-Work-Report.pdf

29. https://www.gov.uk/government/uploads/system/uploads/attachment_data/file/269679/RAGS-lessons-learned-report.pdf

30. http://www.fairtrade.net/single-view+M5fc5b408f70.html—_ftn1

31 Information provided by IKEA to the author, October 2014, publication forthcoming.

32 http://lebasic.com/wp-content/uploads/2014/10/BASIC_German-Banana-Value-Chain-Study_Final.pdf; http://blogs.oxfam.org/en/blogs/14-09-29-aldi-price-it's-time-peel-banana-scandal

33. http://www.relacioneslaborales.gob.ec/wp-content/uploads/2013/12/ACUERDO-MINISTERIAL-0027-SALARIO-DIGNO-PARA-EL-2014.pdf; http://www.lacamara.org/ccg/2013%20Feb%20BE%20CCG%20Salario%20Digno%20y%20las%20PYMES.pdf

34. http://www.camerpost.com/cameroun-le-salaire-minimum-en-hausse-de-pres-de-30-28072014/

35. https://www.tescoplc.com/talkingshop/index.asp?blogid=236.

36. http://www.ethicalteapartnership.org/wp-content/uploads/Raising-Wages-case-study-09.06.14.pdf

37. 'Living Wage Engineering' Fairwear Foundation, http://www.fairwear.org/ul/cms/fck-uploaded/documents/fwfpublications_reports/ LivingWageEngineering20141.pdf

38. http://www.fairwear.org/534/news/news_item/blog-we-can-do-great-things-together--fwfs-ruth-vermeulen-in-turkey/?id=659

39. Interview with the author, September 2014.

40. http://www.theguardian.com/business/2014/sep/21/fashion-retailers-offer-raise-minimum-wage-cambodia

41. http://livingwagecommission.org.uk/wp-content/uploads/2014/06/Work-that-pays_The-Final-Report-of-The-Living-Wage-Commission_w-3.pdf

Organizations to Contact

The editors have compiled the following list of organizations concerned with the issues debated in this book. The descriptions are derived from materials provided by the organizations. All have publications or information available for interested readers. The list was compiled on the date of publication of the present volume; the information provided here may change. Be aware that many organizations take several weeks or longer to respond to inquiries, so allow as much time as possible.

American Enterprise Institute
1789 Massachusetts Avenue NW
Washington, DC 20036
phone: (202) 862-5800
website: www.aei.org

The American Enterprise Institute (AEI) is a public policy think tank dedicated to defending human dignity, expanding human potential, and building a freer and safer world. AEI scholars pursue innovative, independent work across a wide array of subjects. From economics, education, health care, and poverty to foreign and defense studies, public opinion, politics, society, and culture.

CATO Institute
1000 Massachusetts Ave NW
Washington, DC 20001-5403
phone: (202) 842-0200
website: www.cato.org

The Cato Institute is a public policy research organization—a think tank—dedicated to the principles of individual liberty, limited government, free markets, and peace. Its scholars and analysts conduct independent, nonpartisan research on a wide range of policy issues. The mission of the Cato Institute is to originate, disseminate, and increase understanding of public policies based on the principles of individual liberty, limited government, free markets, and peace. Its vision is to create free, open, and civil societies founded on libertarian principles.

Center for American Progress
Center for American Progress
1333 H Street NW, 10th Floor
Washington, DC, 20005
phone: (202) 682-1611
website: www.americanprogress.org

Center for American Progress is an independent nonpartisan policy institute that is dedicated to improving the lives of all Americans through bold, progressive ideas, as well as strong leadership and concerted action. It believes America should be a land of boundless opportunity, where people can climb the ladder of economic mobility. It develops new policy ideas, challenges the media to cover the issues that truly matter, and shapes the national debate.

Economic Policy Institute
1225 Eye Street NW, Suite 600
Washington, DC 20005
phone: (202) 775-8810
email: epi@epi.org
website: www.epi.org

The Economic Policy Institute (EPI) is a nonprofit, nonpartisan think tank created in 1986 to include the needs of low- and middle-income workers in economic policy discussions. EPI conducts research and analysis on the economic status of working America. EPI proposes public policies that protect and improve the economic conditions of low- and middle-income workers and assesses policies with respect to how they affect those workers.

The Heritage Foundation
214 Massachusetts Avenue NE
Washington DC 20002-4999
phone: (202) 546-4400
email: info@heritage.org
website: www.heritage.org

As the nation's largest, most broadly supported conservative research and educational institution—a think tank—the Heritage Foundation has been the bastion of the American conservative movement since its founding in 1973. The Heritage Foundation performs timely, accurate research on key policy issues and effectively marketing these findings to its primary audiences: members of Congress, key congressional staff members, policymakers in the executive branch, the nation's news media, and the academic and policy communities.

National Employment Law Project (NELP)
75 Maiden Lane, #601
New York, NY 10038
phone: (212) 285-3025
email: nelp@nelp.org
website: www.nelp.org

NELP seeks to ensure that America upholds for all workers the promise of opportunity and economic security through work. It publishes research that illuminates workers' issues; promotes policies that improve workers' lives; lends deep legal and policy expertise to important cases and campaigns; and partners with allies to advance crucial reforms.

Pew Research Center
1615 L Street NW, Suite 800
Washington, DC 20036
phone: (202) 419-4300
website: www.pewsocialtrends.org

The Pew Research Center is a nonpartisan fact tank that informs the public about the issues, attitudes, and trends shaping America and the world. It conducts public opinion polling, demographic research, media content analysis, and other empirical social science research. Pew Research Center does not take policy positions.

Political Economy Research Institute
Gordon Hall, 418 N. Pleasant Street, Suite A
Amherst, MA 01002
phone: (413) 545-6355
email: peri@peri.umass.edu
website: www.peri.umass.edu

PERI is an independent unit of the University of Massachusetts, Amherst, with close ties to the Department of Economics. PERI staff frequently work collaboratively with faculty members and graduate students from the University of Massachusetts, and other economists from around the world. PERI is a leading source of research and policy initiatives on issues of globalization, unemployment, financial market instability, central bank policy, living wages and decent work, and the economics of peace, development, and the environment.

Bibliography

Books

Dale Belman and Paul J. Wolfson. *What Does the Minimum Wage Do?* Kalamazoo, MI: Upjohn Institute Press, 2014.

David Card and Alan B. Krueger. *Myth and Measurement: The New Economics of the Minimum Wage*. Princeton, NJ: Princeton University Press, 2015.

Deborah M. Figart , Ellen Mutari, and Marilyn Power. *Living Wages, Equal Wages: Gender and Labor Market Policies in the United States*. New York, NY: Routledge Press, 2002.

Willis J. Nordlund. *The Quest for a Living Wage: The History of the Federal Minimum Wage Program*. Westport, CT: Greenwood Publishing Group, 1997.

Robert Polund and Stephanie Luce. *The Living Wage: Building a Fair Economy*. New York, NY: The New Press, 1998.

Robert Polund. *A Measure of Fairness: The Economics of Living Wages and Minimum Wages in the United States*. Ithaca, NY: Cornell University Press, 2008.

William Quigley. *Ending Poverty s We Know It: Guaranteeing a Right to a Job*. Philadelphia, PA: Temple University Press, 2003.

David Rolf. *The Fight for Fifteen: The Right Wage for a Working America*. New York, NY: The New Press, 2016.

Donald Staible. *Political Economy of a Living Wage: Progressives, the New Deal, and Social Justice*. New York, NY: Palgrave Macmillan, 2016.

Richard R. Troxell. *Looking Up at the Bottom Line. The Struggle for the Living Wage!*. Austin, TX: Plain View Press, 2010.

Periodicals and Internet Sources

http://minimum-wage.procon.org

http://livingwage.mit.edu

Vanessa Cárdenas. "The Benefits of Increasing the Minimum Wage for People of Color," Center for American Progress, April 21 2014, https://www.americanprogress.org/issues/

race/news/2014/04/21/87248/the-benefits-of-increasing-the-minimum-wage-for-people-of-color.

Jeffrey Clemens and Michael Wither. "The Minimum Wage and the Great Recession: Evidence on the Employment and Income Trajectories of Low-Skilled Workers," National Bureau of Economic Research, November 2014, http://www.nber.org/papers/w20724.

Benjamin H. Harris and Melissa S. Kearney. "The 'Ripple Effect' of a Minimum Wage Increase on American Workers," www.brookings.com, January 10, 2014, https://www.brookings.edu/blog/up-front/2014/01/10/the-ripple-effect-of-a-minimum-wage-increase-on-american-workers.

Don Lee. "Four Consequences of a $15 Minimum Wage," *Los Angeles Times*, April 25, 2016, http://www.latimes.com/business/la-fi-minimum-wage-impacts-20160421-snap-htmlstory.html.

Dylan Matthews. "A $15 Minimum Wage Is a Terrible Idea," *Washington Post*, June 22, 2013, https://www.washingtonpost.com/news/wonk/wp/2013/06/22/a-15-minimum-wage-is-a-terrible-idea/?utm_term=.bbe00d2ebd77.

David Neumark and William Wascher. "Minimum Wage and Employment: A Review of Evidence from the New Minimum Wage Research," National Bureau of Economic Research, November 2006, http://www.nber.org/papers/w12663.

Robert Reich. "Why the Minimum Wage Should Really Be Raised to $15 an Hour," RobertReich.org, April 8, 2014, http://robertreich.org/post/82134788482.

Sita Slavov and Aspen Gorry. "Minimum Wage, Maximum Harm," *US News & World Report*, May 1, 2014, https://www.usnews.com/opinion/economic-intelligence/2014/05/01/a-minimum-wage-hike-would-hurt-young-workers-worse-than-cbo-estimated.

Index

Economic Policy Institute, 18, 57,
 142, 143
Elmore, Andrew, 131
Ergon Associates, 186
Ethical Tea Partnership, 186
Ethical Trading Initiative (ETI), 184

F

Fair Labor Standards Act (FLSA), 7,
 17, 28, 74–75, 78, 79
Fair Minimum Wage Act, 49, 50,
 51–52, 90, 139, 140, 143
Fairphone, 184
Fairris, David, 120, 122, 125, 127
Fair Trade, 184
Fairtrade International, 186
Fair Wage Network, 181, 185, 187
Fairwear Foundation (FWF),
 186–187
Federal Reserve Bank of Chicago, 82
Federal Reserve Board, 15, 38, 56
"Fight for $15," 66, 147–148
Food and Agriculture Organization
 (FAO), 185
Fortin, Nicole, 56
Freedom of Association, 184
Freeman, Richard, 125
Friedman, Milton, 77

G

Gap, 184
Gilroy, Curtis, 79
Gindling, Tim (T.H.), 151–164
Government Accountability Office
 (GAO), 35–36
  Great Depression, 10, 141
Great Recession, 52, 102, 112, 113
Greenberg Quinlan Rosner
 Research, 143

H

Hall, Doug, 89–105
H&M, 187

Harkin, Tom, 90, 140
Healthy Families Act, 54
HELP Committee, 28
Heritage Foundation, 28
Hired Labour Standard, 184
Hirsch, Barry, 55, 81
Howell, David, 66–72
Howes, Candace, 123

I

Ikea, 185
ILO Constitution, 179
Imani Development, 186
Impactt, 183
Inditex, 183
IndustriALL, 188
Innovations for Poverty Action, 55
International Framework
 Agreement, 183
International Union of Food,
 Agricultural, Hotel, Restaurant,
 Catering, Tobacco and Allied
 Workers' Associations (IUF),
 186
ISEAL Alliance, 184

J

Jim Crow, 65
Joint Economic Committee, 80

K

Kahn, Shulamit, 40
Katz, Carla A., 147–150
Kaufman, Bruce, 55
Kennedy, Edward, 18
Keynes, John Maynard, 11, 13
Klein, Ezra, 16
Kohen, Andrew, 79
Kosters, Marvin, 77
Krueger, Alan, 13, 14, 54

31901061000230